Fly Girls

Fly Girls

THE DARING AMERICAN
WOMEN PILOTS WHO
HELPED WIN WWII

P. O'CONNELL PEARSON

Simon & Schuster Books for Young Readers

NEW YORK   LONDON   TORONTO   SYDNEY   NEW DELHI

SIMON & SCHUSTER BOOKS FOR YOUNG READERS

An imprint of Simon & Schuster Children's Publishing Division

1230 Avenue of the Americas, New York, New York 10020

SIMON & SCHUSTER BOOKS FOR YOUNG READERS

is a trademark of Simon & Schuster, Inc.

For information about special discounts for bulk purchases, please contact Simon & Schuster Special Sales at 1-866-506-1949 or business@simonandschuster.com.

The Simon & Schuster Speakers Bureau can bring authors to your live event. For more information or to book an event, contact the Simon & Schuster Speakers Bureau at 1-866-248-3049 or visit our website at www.simonspeakers.com.

Jacket design by Chloë Foglia | Interior design by Hilary Zarycky

Map art by Drew Willis

The text for this book was set in New Caledonia.

Manufactured in the United States of America | 0118 FFG

First Edition

2 4 6 8 10 9 7 5 3 1

Library of Congress Cataloging-in-Publication Data

Names: Pearson, P. O'Connell (Patricia O'Connell), author.

Title: Fly girls : the daring American women pilots who helped win WWII / P. O'Connell Pearson.

Description: First edition. | New York : Simon & Schuster Books for Young Readers, 2018. | Audience: Age: 10 and up. | Audience: Grade: 7 to 8.

Identifiers: LCCN 2017011062 | ISBN 9781534404106 (hardcover) | ISBN 9781534404120 (eBook)

Subjects: LCSH: Women Airforce Service Pilots (U.S.)—Juvenile literature. | Women air pilots—United States—Juvenile literature. | Air pilots, Military—United States—Juvenile literature. | World War, 1939–1945—Aerial operations, American—Juvenile literature. | World War, 1939–1945—Participation, Female—Juvenile literature.

Classification: LCC D790 .P394 2018 | DDC 940.54/497309252—dc23

LC record available at https://lccn.loc.gov/2017011062

For my father

ACKNOWLEDGMENTS

In the course of writing this book I have developed tremendous appreciation for all the women of the WAFS and WASP, and am grateful to them for what they did between 1942 and 1944 and for their letters, memoirs, autobiographies, oral interviews, and more. They continue to inspire.

My thanks to the Experimental Aircraft Association AirVenture and museum in Oshkosh, Wisconsin, and to the staff and volunteers in Manassas, Virginia, who gave graciously of their time and expertise and even allowed me to sit in the cockpit of the B-17 Aluminum Overcast. Their enthusiasm for the WASP is wonderful. My thanks also to Carol Cain at the National WASP World War II Museum in Sweetwater, Texas.

A special thanks to Sarah Byrn Rickman, who shared her font of knowledge and her passion for educating others on the WAFS and WASP. Her attention to the smallest detail made the book better. And Liz Kossnar at Simon & Schuster guided me with great patience and acted as a cheerleader at the same time. I am indebted to Susan E. Goodman and Chris Lynch for their ongoing mentorship and guidance that goes far beyond the call of duty, and for their friendship. Finally, my love and gratitude to my husband, Paul, whose constant support is unfailing.

CONTENTS

1. War Clouds
1

2. Preparing For War
15

3. No More Choices
29

4. Answering the Call
47

5. Becoming Wasps
61

6. Ferrying for Uncle Sam
81

7. Yes to Every Job
97

8. Greater Heights
115

9. Attacked
137

10. At Last
157

Epilogue
173

Bibliography
178

Notes
183

Time Line
189

Index
192

A night view of the 1939 New York World's Fair—"World of Tomorrow."

CHAPTER 1

War Clouds

★

President Franklin D. Roosevelt stood in front of a well-dressed crowd. His legs, paralyzed by polio years before, were held stiff with braces and hidden behind a large podium. Rain threatened on this April morning, but the president stuck out his chin and smiled in his usual way. Roosevelt was in New York for a happy event—the opening of the 1939 New York World's Fair, an exhibition of new ideas and innovations for the "World of Tomorrow." The *New York Times* reported, PRESIDENT OPENS FAIR AS A SYMBOL OF PEACE.[1] Everyone knew about the predictions of war in Europe. The radio news was full of Adolf Hitler's threats and military aggression every night. But while the president may have been worried about dictators and wars, he understood that visitors to the world's fair were far more interested in dazzling new technologies and a bit of fun. In his brief remarks FDR mentioned peace and American prayers for an end to strife in Europe, but he didn't dwell on those ideas.

The 1930s had been an economic disaster in the United

Causes of World War II

During the 1920s and 1930s, dictators gained control in several countries, including Germany and Italy. In Japan a group of military leaders gained the powers of a dictator. Dictators have complete power. They are not limited by constitutions, laws, courts, or elections, and can use their nation's military to control people. These three totalitarian governments—Germany, Italy, and Japan—were called the Axis. Their people did not have freedom of speech or the right to fair trials. There were no elections, and the government controlled newspapers and radio. The Axis powers built huge militaries and promoted the glory of war. They also promoted extreme nationalism—the belief that their countries and peoples were better than other countries and peoples— and felt they had the right to take over weaker nations (which is called imperialism). The world's strong democratic countries did almost nothing to stop them. Totalitarianism, militarism, extreme nationalism, and imperialism in the Axis nations were major causes of World War II.

States and around the world. After the stock market crashed in 1929, banks closed, businesses shut down, and millions of people lost their jobs and homes. That kind of economic slowdown is called a depression, and this, the Great Depression, had been the worst in history. Roosevelt and the people in his administration had worked tirelessly to ease the misery Americans suffered, yet the Great Depression wasn't over. Finally, though, businesses had started hiring again, and now more people could afford to buy a few things and relax a little—exactly what they wanted to do. Whatever the radio said about conflicts and threats in Europe, problems three thousand miles away had nothing to do with the United States, they thought. In America it was time to dream a little and look forward to a better decade ahead.

When Roosevelt declared the fair officially "open to all mankind," a cheer went up from the dignitaries. Then ordinary fairgoers streamed into the park—more than two hundred thousand on the first day alone—having paid their fifty-cent admission and ready to see what the "World of Tomorrow" might look like.

Massive halls filled with elaborate displays from companies including General Motors, Ford, and Westinghouse showed off plans for the future. Before long, regular houses would have marvels like electric refrigerators with freezers, quick-to-cook frozen foods, and dishwashers. Women were promised they'd be able to finish fixing dinner and doing the dishes and still look like the model in the display—"as neat and refreshed as when she started."[2] Those new houses would have air-conditioning, too, and even televisions. In fact, the president's speech that very morning was the first event ever broadcast on television. The television audience, of course, was almost nonexistent, since companies like RCA and General Electric were just introducing the television at the fair. Everyone wanted to see the display models, but television sales wouldn't take off for another decade.

Visitors to the fair saw more than household goods in their future. They learned that in just twenty years, by 1960, they'd travel in hover cars zipping at 100 miles per hour above high-speed roadways crisscrossing the country in every direction. Even more amazing, ordinary people would soon be able to travel great distances by air.

Air travel wasn't new in 1939. Anyone over the age of forty could remember the reports of the Wright brothers' first airplane in 1903. They'd seen pictures of the amazing flight at Kitty Hawk, North Carolina. The airplane had seemed like a glorious toy at the time, and in some ways it still did, though flying had come a long way in the few decades since then.

During the Great War—what we call World War I—dashing pilots in tiny aircraft had introduced a new kind of warfare and captured the imaginations of people around the country and the world. When the war ended in 1918, most of those people tried to forget the horrible number of deaths and terrible destruction the war had caused. They vowed never to repeat such a thing. But their fascination with the quick little airplanes and heroic pilots who flew them remained.

Many of those pilots continued to fly after the war as barn-stormers, holding shows at fairgrounds and in open fields. The sound of their happily buzzing engines let people in towns know they'd arrived. Whole families trooped to wherever the pilots

Charles Lindbergh and Amelia Earhart

Charles Lindbergh was the first pilot to fly solo from New York to Paris. He made his transatlantic crossing in 1927 in a tiny plane called the *Spirit of St. Louis*. Several other pilots had already tried and failed to cross the Atlantic, so the whole world followed news of Lindbergh's flight and cheered his success. Lindbergh was handsome, clean cut, polite, and humble—traits that made him an instant hero.

Five years later Amelia Earhart became the first woman pilot to fly solo across the Atlantic Ocean. There had been other daring women pilots who made news, but Earhart—who was tall, thin, and fresh-faced like Lindbergh—had the same kind of soft-spoken, polite humility he did and won people's hearts as well as their admiration. She used her fame to promote aviation and women's rights and opportunities. While attempting to make a flight around the world in 1937, Earhart and her navigator, Fred Noonan, disappeared near Howland Island in the Pacific. No evidence of their crash has ever been found, though searches still continue today.

had set down to watch the daredevil performances. Pilots spun straight down toward the earth, pulling their planes up at the last possible second, the crowd gasping in shock. They rolled lazily through the sky as if they never got dizzy. For a fee, a brave spectator could go up for a short ride. When barnstormer and mail pilot Charles Lindbergh flew alone across the Atlantic Ocean in 1927, he became an instant hero worldwide. And everyone worried and then wept when aviator Amelia Earhart disappeared over the Pacific ten years later.

A lot of young people—boys and girls—watched those shows and wished they could be pilots. They dreamed of seeing the world from above and going farther, faster, and higher than anyone ever had. The Depression had stifled an awful lot of dreams, but not flight. By the time visitors to the New York World's Fair were staring openmouthed at the cockpit of a passenger plane in 1939, some of those young dreamers were licensed pilots and logging as many hours in the air as possible. Only a few people, most of them men, actually made a living as pilots. The others flew small one- or two-seater aircraft for the sheer joy of flying.

Most people in 1939, of course, may have liked watching planes, but they had never traveled by plane or even considered the possibility. So when visitors to the world's fair climbed the stairs into one of the first commercial planes anywhere— an American Airlines passenger plane—they saw a remarkable future. Very soon multiple passengers would sit in cushy seats while pretty, perhaps glamorous, women in crisp suits and high heels brought them food and drinks, like elegantly uniformed waitresses in a nice restaurant, as they flew across the Atlantic Ocean. *Amazing*. Even more astonishing were the mind-boggling controls, dials, and levers visitors stared at in the cockpit of the sleek silver plane. How did the handsome men in almost-military uniforms learn to operate such a complex machine? How did they have the nerve to try?

In Washington, DC, that spring General Henry "Hap" Arnold was thinking about the future of flight too. Arnold's interest in flying, though, was work, not play. In fact, he was working harder than was good for his blood pressure, but he couldn't see a way to slow down. Not in 1939.

A career military man with over thirty years in the army, Arnold had taken flying lessons from Orville and Wilbur Wright in 1911. He was an expert on aviation and had studied the way airplanes were used in the Great War. He concluded that bigger, more powerful planes would be key to winning any future war. He had a hard time convincing very many people to listen to his ideas, though. Military leaders didn't want to think about a completely new way of fighting. And most of Congress and the American people wanted nothing to do with building the military during the 1920s and 1930s. They'd been shocked by the horror of the Great War and were determined to avoid any more international conflicts. Besides, the Great Depression had used up every financial resource the country had, so there was no money for aircraft or pilots anyway.

As the threat of war increased in Europe, though, Franklin Roosevelt listened to and believed Hap Arnold and persuaded lawmakers that the armed forces had to modernize and grow. Congress passed legislation to increase the military budget, and Hap Arnold was appointed head of the Army Air Corps. Arnold seemed to smile a bit all the time. But when it came to building an air force, he was deadly serious. He and FDR asked Congress for money to build ten thousand planes. Congress okayed six thousand.

It was a start. Yet Arnold worried that the country had dragged its feet for too long. How much time would it take to build those planes? How long to train thousands of pilots? How soon would they be needed? From Arnold's desk the world of tomorrow didn't look nearly as bright as the world's fair promised.

• • •

Meanwhile, in New Jersey, a young woman named Ann Baumgartner was trying to decide what to do with her life. Ann had graduated from Smith College in June with a degree in premed. That was a bold choice for a woman in 1939, since less than 10 percent of doctors were women at the time. Ann wasn't afraid of bold choices, but she wanted a break before deciding about medical school. Her mother suggested she sail to Europe and then they would meet in England for a visit to their British relatives while she considered her choices. Ann had aunts, uncles, and cousins in England and had always enjoyed her stays with them. Being able to see the great art museums of Italy and France as well . . . what could be better? This trip, however, wasn't what she expected.

> At each port we visited . . . I felt the deep hatred
> Hitler had already engendered. . . .
> . . . Nazis spoke confidently in loud voices, played
> loud music, drank, and sang loud songs, while the
> Europeans glanced at them with hatred . . . When
> the ship stopped at Venice . . . I saw . . . a marching
> column, circling the square, singing and clapping
> loudly. . . .
> Later I came to recognize, and fear, that
> marching song in other European towns.[3]

In England there were no Nazis to deal with, yet Ann could feel the growing tension Hitler was causing. She walked in the countryside and watched her aunts play croquet and tend their rosebushes while fear seeped through the warm air. Hitler had made and broken many promises as he took control of ever more territory in Europe, and England and France gave in to his demands again and again to avoid war. Neither country was fully recovered from the Great War, and they weren't prepared to fight

Adolf Hitler and the Nazi Party

The Nazi Party was founded in Germany soon after World War I. Its leader was Adolf Hitler. Hitler promoted extreme pride in Germany and absolute loyalty to his dictatorship. He encouraged racism based on the

belief that "true" Germans—he called them Aryans—were tall, blond, blue eyed, physically fit, and superior to other people. He blamed Germany's problems on Jews in particular, as well as minorities, the disabled, and others who didn't fit the Aryan model (this is called scapegoating). His powerful speeches convinced many Germans to support discrimination and the takeover of neighboring countries. Hitler was largely responsible for the outbreak of World War II and for the murder of over six million Jews and other targets of Nazi hate in the Holocaust.

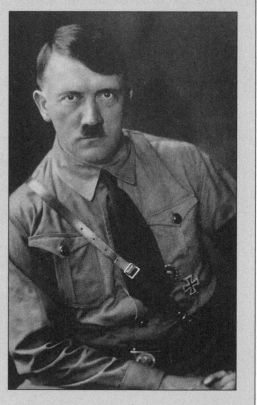

again so soon. But they had vowed to defend Poland if Hitler invaded.

Every night news of Germany's advances sent Ann's uncles and cousin, all government men, behind closed doors for hushed phone calls and discussions. Her aunts were distant and distracted while they tried to play cards or make conversation. The Great War had been devastating. It seemed an entire generation of young men had died. Another war could be even worse.

On Friday, September 1, the news everyone dreaded came across the radio. German armies had invaded Poland.

Ann's family spent the weekend in a tense quiet. They knew all the men in the family would be called on if Britain went to war. They knew how unprepared the country was. Some newsmen joked without humor that England had "four good rifles and three good planes to defend herself" against the German war machine.[4] The waiting was miserable as the whole country held its breath.

On Sunday the wait was over. Prime Minister Neville Chamberlain addressed the nation over the radio, sounding tired and terribly sad. He spoke very briefly. What was there to say? Only one sentence mattered. "I have to tell you . . . this country is at war with Germany."[5]

A frightening stillness fell throughout Great Britain. It seemed no one dared to speak, as if so long as no one said anything or caught another person's eye, if they didn't breathe too loudly or move, they could hang on to the last moment of peace and postpone the beginning of war. In fact, war had already begun.

A day later Ann and her mother boarded a horribly over-crowded Danish refugee ship with hundreds of other people trying to get home to America. Ann hated leaving her British family, but her uncle Vernon had insisted.

Fifty mattresses covered the floor of a big room on the main deck, and trying to sleep only six inches from a perfect stranger's snoring was difficult. Worse, the three nearest toilets overflowed onto the floor beneath some mattresses. Though the smell was awful, the discomfort was nothing compared with the worry that spread with reports of another refugee ship being hit and sunk by a German submarine, a U-boat.

Ann helped paint all the ship's portholes black so lights couldn't be seen by other ships or U-boats. Days and nights crawled by. No one could bathe. Food and drinking water ran short and then vanished. Passengers didn't feel safe until the Statue of Liberty appeared on the horizon.[6]

As desperately glad as she was to be home and out of danger, Ann couldn't stop thinking about what her uncle had said as he told her good-bye.

> If you want to help, then work to persuade your
> country to help us supply ourselves with what we'll
> need. Though your president sees our need, his
> Congress and your people are not behind him. You
> must help.[7]

Ann promised herself she would somehow help Great Britain against the horror of Hitler. And not just for her family. If the United States didn't help, democracy might be destroyed in Europe. If democracy died there, it could very well die everywhere, even in America.

Nancy Love with her plane, circa 1930.

CHAPTER 2

Preparing for War

J acqueline Cochran understood more about aviation than most people could imagine. She was an accomplished pilot who owned her own plane, and in 1938 she won the Bendix Trophy Race by flying from California to Ohio faster than any other pilot, man or woman. Cochran was only the second woman to achieve the title—Louise Thaden, with copilot Blanche Noyes, won in 1938—and Cochran's win made news.

Cochran made news again in March 1939 when she set an altitude record for American women flyers by reaching thirty-three thousand feet. That achievement left her with a terrible headache for days because of the changes in oxygen and pressure, and a temperature of sixty degrees below zero. But Jackie Cochran craved adventure and added the altitude record to the pile of trophies and awards she'd accumulated when she wasn't busy running her very successful cosmetics business. She liked being busy, loved flying, and basked in all the attention.

Dashing around the country didn't keep Jackie from hearing

the same news of war in Europe that everyone else did. Unlike many Americans, however, she believed the United States could not and should not ignore the conflicts there. Cochran and President Franklin Roosevelt had almost nothing in common, but they agreed that it was past time to build America's military, especially the Army Air Corps. And if Americans were pulled into another war . . . well . . . Jacqueline Cochran wanted to use her skills and brains for something bigger than collecting trophies.

Like Hap Arnold and FDR, Cochran thought about how long it took to build planes and knew a bit about how long it took to train pilots. She came up with a plan to help. And once Jackie had a plan, another woman pilot said, "She'd figure out a way to get what she wanted."[8]

Long before she learned to fly, Cochran had learned determination—some people called her stubborn. Growing up in rural Florida, she didn't have much money or schooling, but she made up her mind very early that she was going to *be* somebody. As a teen, she learned to style hair and then moved to New York City. She'd given herself an interesting life story by then—and the name Jacqueline. Much better than the Bessie she'd grown up with, she thought. Always beautifully dressed and oozing confidence, Jackie landed a job with a very expensive hair salon, and by the early 1930s she had a list of rich and influential customers. But what she really wanted was to be her own boss and become one of those rich and influential people herself. She decided to start a cosmetics company.

In the days before social media or television, people trying to sell something like a new beauty product traveled to individual salons around the country. They'd demonstrate the product and try to convince salon owners to use it and offer it for sale. Jackie knew so much travel wasn't going to be easy. And she faced plenty of competition and an economic depression. None of those obstacles stopped Cochran. At an elegant Miami dinner she explained to the wealthy businessman sitting next to her what she had in mind. Floyd Odlum liked her business idea but said that if she wanted to make money in such a difficult economic climate, she'd "need wings." Traveling by air would allow her to cover far more territory than most other salespeople did, he told her. "Get your pilot's license."[9]

Just weeks later Cochran had her pilot's license and a new passion. As she put it, "When I paid for my first lesson, a beauty operator ceased to exist and an aviator was born."[10]

Jackie continued to work on building her business and also began competing in air races. Within a few years Jacqueline Cochran Cosmetics was successful, Jackie and Floyd were married, and Cochran was collecting flying prizes, flying titles, and flying records one on top of the other. In 1938 she won the Harmon Trophy as the world's outstanding woman pilot of the year (a men's trophy was awarded as well). She won the Harmon again in 1939, this time with an additional honor: First Lady Eleanor Roosevelt presented the trophy to Jackie at a ceremony in Washington, DC.[11]

Cochran didn't hesitate to point out her aviation accomplishments (as of 2017, Cochran still held more speed, distance, and altitude records than any pilot before or after her—man or woman), but she faced criticism for boasting. Men could brag a bit; women shouldn't. Jackie said she was the best anyway. Yet she recognized there were other very capable woman pilots too. As the threat of war in Europe grew, she considered what they could offer if the United States became involved. Jackie believed women could do a dozen noncombat flying jobs that military pilots were doing on bases in the United States, freeing hundreds if not thousands of men for combat flying. But she faced criticism for saying that, too.

Cochran got nowhere when she wrote to the military about her idea. She wasn't surprised. Women could be strong and independent, but they didn't do military things. During the Great War, women who wanted to volunteer to fly for the army were told no. Military leaders rejected the idea again in the early 1930s. Such a thing, one said, was "utterly unfeasible" since *all* women were "high strung," which means "nervous."[12]

In late September 1939, about three weeks after Europe fell into war, Cochran wrote another letter saying such a plan "requires organizing in advance." Waiting for a war to begin made no sense. Cochran didn't send her letter to the military this time. She didn't even send it to the president. Instead she sent it to the First Lady, knowing Mrs. Roosevelt would remember meeting her earlier in the year.[13]

Eleanor Roosevelt was a strong supporter of women's rights and equality, and she had a big audience. She traveled and spoke everywhere, had her own radio program, and wrote a daily newspaper column. Cochran got an encouraging response from Mrs. Roosevelt, though both women knew only the military could make the decision.

In Boston another experienced pilot, named Nancy Love, was also thinking about war and women pilots. Nancy was a member of the Ninety-Nines, a club for women flyers whose first president had been Amelia Earhart. The club, founded in 1929, was named for its original ninety-nine members. By 1939 over four hundred women pilots belonged. (Today thousands of women around the world are members of the Ninety-Nines.) Nancy had earned her pilot's license at sixteen, had a degree from Vassar College, and worked as a pilot for the company her husband, also a pilot, had started. She and other women pilots had even been hired by the federal government to go across the country convincing local officials to paint their towns' names on distinctive rooftops as navigation points for pilots, since planes didn't have radar in those days.

In early 1940, Nancy wrote a letter to Colonel Robert Olds, then head of the Plans Division of the Army Air Corps. Love knew there were many piloting jobs to be done outside of combat and that women could fly as well as men in those jobs. She already had a list of names ready, names of women she knew to be "excellent material."[14] However, Olds didn't need more pilots in the Army Air Corps in 1940—he needed more planes. Still, he didn't completely reject Love's idea and kept her letter on file in case the situation changed. Any final decision, though, would have to be made by the Army Air Corps chief of staff, General Hap Arnold.

How Planes Fly

Airplanes are large, heavy objects. A plane's weight will always pull it toward Earth. But a plane's wings are designed to produce lift. When the plane is moving, the shape of the wings forces more air over the wing than under it. This creates greater pressure beneath the wing than above it, causing the plane to move upward against the force of gravity. Think of an umbrella on a windy day. If it is held straight, the wind can cause it to rise upward. This is lift—different from what happens when the umbrella is held at an angle and the wind blows it inside out.

The plane's size will always create drag, or resistance to moving forward through the air. The plane moves forward because the propellers cause the air in front of them to flow faster than the air behind them. This shifts the air pressure, just as the wings do, but creates forward instead of upward lift, called thrust. The plane is propelled (some scientists say it is pulled, others say pushed) forward as long as the thrust is greater than the drag.

A plane's controls allow the pilot to steer the aircraft by tilting the plane so that one wing is higher than the other. This causes a banked, or curved, flight path. The rudder—somewhat like a paddle—is hinged to the rear of the vertical section of the plane's tail and keeps the plane's nose in line with the banked flight path. High winds or turbulence makes maintaining a smooth path difficult.

Nancy's suggestion didn't get any farther than Jackie's had. For one thing, Hap Arnold agreed with Olds that what the Army Air Corps needed was more planes, not more pilots. And while he believed there were a lot of skilled women pilots out there, he wasn't convinced a "slip of a young girl" could fly an enormous bomber or transport plane, especially in bad weather.[15] Arnold had experience flying those heavy planes and knew the foot pedals a pilot used to operate the rudders on the plane's tail took enormous leg strength. The control wheel or stick could exhaust the strongest man's arms in high wind.[16] Women, he thought, simply weren't strong enough. Nancy Love disagreed and continued to look for qualified women for her list.

The spring of 1940 brought new crowds to the New York World's Fair (a total of forty million people attended before it was over). Yet the fair seemed to lose some of its glitter with the news that Nazi armies had invaded Denmark and Norway in April and crashed through Belgium, Luxembourg, and the Netherlands in May. In early June, France fell to German forces, and Great Britain almost lost an entire army trapped on the French coast at Dunkirk as the Germans advanced. Thankfully, most of the 350,000 men were rescued at the last possible minute. Even so, Hitler was sure the British would give up any day. Newly elected prime minister Winston Churchill, who sounded like he'd swallowed gravel and looked like a big-bellied bulldog, stood firm. "We shall never surrender," he told the world. But how?

Allies Versus Axis

By 1939 the world had broken into two camps. Germany, Italy, and Japan were called the Axis and had support from a small number of other countries. The world's democracies, led by Great Britain, France, and eventually the United States, as well as another sixty nations, were known as the Allies. The Soviet Union or USSR (today's Russia was the largest part of the USSR) was a communist country but also joined the Allies against the Axis and played a major role in winning the war.

Churchill admitted that a staggering number of lives would be lost in the struggle. Already tens of thousands of British men were dead. Ann Baumgartner would soon get the news that her cousin Geoffrey was one of them—killed at Dunkirk. Eventually her two uncles would be killed as well.[17] For many Americans, the horror of what was happening in Europe began to sink in.

Churchill managed to inspire confidence in the British people, who wondered if their small island nation could possibly defeat the Nazis. The prime minister insisted that somehow Britain would "carry on the struggle, until . . . the New World, with all its power and might, steps forth to the rescue and the liberation of the old."[18]

Canadian and some Australian pilots were already flying with the British Royal Air Force (RAF). Help with ground forces would follow. But neither Canada nor Australia had a large population or vast industries. President Roosevelt knew exactly what the prime minister was saying. The "New World, with all its power and might" included the military and industrial strength of the United States. Britain needed that power and might. Fast.

Throughout the summer American newspapers reported on the terrible battle being fought in the skies over England. Night after night German planes dropped bombs on British cities, destroying buildings, bridges, and railroads, and killing innocent civilians. The RAF scrambled to defend the country against the German bombers. Young British pilots with little training and even less sleep risked everything to keep Germany from forcing Britain to surrender. The losses were unthinkable, but the British pilots had an advantage. Their fighter planes were faster and more maneuverable than the German bombers. Finally Hitler had to admit that his plan to bomb the island of Great Britain into submission wasn't going to work. He would have to find a new strategy. For the time being, at least, Britain's pilots and planes—its airpower—had saved the British nation.

In the United States, meanwhile, Congress acted to increase the size of the army. At the time, the US Army had less than two hundred thousand men. It was smaller than the armies of at least fifteen other countries.[19] Congress passed a conscription act—what we usually call the draft—allowing the government to require young men to join the military. Roosevelt signed it into law. FDR also met with leaders of industry about how factories might shift from producing cars and washing machines to making tanks and military aircraft. The luxuries those industries were finally selling again after ten years of the Depression would have to wait.

Roosevelt couldn't force businesses to plan for a war that didn't exist yet. But he could ask questions and encourage industry to ask itself those questions. How long would it take to convert an auto plant into a tank plant? Could a factory making women's silk stockings make silk parachutes instead? Might bacon grease lubricate machine parts if other oil couldn't be found? And how could the United States, which had declared neutrality at the start of the war in Europe, help protect democracy in a world that dictators were determined to conquer?

In March 1941 both Jacqueline Cochran and General Hap Arnold attended a White House aviation awards luncheon in Washington, DC. Jackie was always ready to promote her ideas and took advantage of the opportunity to talk to General Arnold about her proposal for women pilots. Though Arnold still believed the United States had enough male pilots, he knew Great Britain was using women to ferry planes from factories to bases. They were doing well and he was rethinking his opinion of women pilots. The United States was about to start sending new bombers to England to replace those being lost in battle. Arnold suggested to Jackie that she go there, see how the British women's program worked, and maybe even recruit American women to join the British.[20]

For Jackie, it was a step in the right direction. In June, Cochran arrived in London in a bomber she'd flown across the Atlantic Ocean. As the lead pilot in command of an all-male crew, she proved a woman could, in fact, fly a heavy plane over long distances. Getting into the air hadn't been easy, though. "Red tape and sexist insinuations stood mountainously in my way," she said later.[21] While she was preparing in the United States, the officers in charge had insisted she take off and land over and over to prove she could manage a big plane. They didn't care that she had set seventeen aviation records. Even after all the testing, the men ordered a male pilot to land the plane in England because Jackie had mentioned that her arm was tired after all those landings in one day.[22]

Those men probably didn't think they were discriminating or being sexist. It was the way they'd thought for their whole lives.

Soviet Women Fly in Combat

The Soviet Union, one of the Allied powers, established three all-women flying squadrons during World War II. Pilots, crew, technicians, mechanics—all were women. And all three squadrons flew combat missions. The most famous squadron was the 588th Night Bomber Regiment—called the Night Witches by German forces. They flew some thirty thousand nighttime bombing missions against German forces.*

But on the day Cochran and her crew were to head for England, she found the pilot's window smashed and the oxygen system tampered with. Someone was so opposed to a woman piloting a big plane, he was willing to resort to sabotage.[23] Though Jackie and the crew were delayed, she wasn't about to quit.

Once in England, Cochran discovered that British women were flying every kind of military plane from factories to bases just as men were. Moreover, when German bombers appeared, the women raced for the tarmac and into danger as fast as the men. Their job was to get as many planes as possible off the ground to protect them from bombs. Those planes weren't armed, so all the women could do was dodge the air battle until it was safe to land and hope they weren't hit. Sometimes hope didn't work, and Jackie realized those women had more courage than most people ever would.

Cochran began recruiting top-notch American women pilots to join the British Air Transport Auxiliary (ATA). She was honest with them about the dangers and discomforts they would face.

They'd have no heating, no warm water, and poor food, in addition to being shot at. That didn't scare the women off. At least in England, they could aid the war effort. As one American woman who wished she could join Jackie said, "Flying is my only talent and one which is in great demand now."[24]

In the meantime, Nancy Love hadn't given up on her plan to recruit women pilots either. Quietly she continued searching aviation records for women with impressive flying experience. She hoped to find women with enough skill and time in the air to adapt to military planes very quickly. They needed to be ready fast if war came to the United States. And Love was certain it would.

The USS *Shaw* **explodes during the Japanese raid on Pearl Harbor on December 7, 1941.**

CHAPTER 3
No More Choices

★

On a beautiful Sunday morning in early December 1941, Cornelia Fort left her apartment in Waikiki, a neighborhood on the beach in Honolulu, Hawaii. It was a short drive to the nearby airport where she worked as a flight instructor and pilot for tourists who paid to see the Hawaiian Islands from the air. Not many women did that kind of work, and some people let Cornelia know it wasn't proper work for a young lady. She didn't mind. Cornelia loved flying and was used to doing things her own way.

Cornelia Fort had grown up on her wealthy family's estate near Nashville, Tennessee. As a young girl, the long-legged, wildly curly-haired Cornelia was a daredevil. She sometimes stood on her pony's bare back while riding and liked to roughhouse or play Tarzan with her three older brothers. When she got older, she hated having to "fuss and carry on" about her appearance, though she learned to be a proper "Southern belle." She dressed well, played golf and tennis, and always displayed the good manners her parents insisted on. There wasn't much room in a Southern belle's life for adventure, and as Cornelia finished school, she decided she had to break away.[25]

One afternoon in early 1940, a friend dating a pilot asked Cornelia to come along for a plane ride. Cornelia had never flown but figured it might be fun to go up. Before the little plane reached cruising altitude, Cornelia Fort was in love with flying. By the time the plane landed, she knew she had to get a pilot's license. She thought the only thing better than flying as a passenger would be flying as a pilot. By fall Fort had her pilot's license, and a few months later she qualified as an instructor. She knew about the women flying for the RAF in England and had no doubt American women could do the same thing if they were allowed to. In the meantime, she started applying for flight instructor jobs anywhere and everywhere, though she was afraid no flight school would hire a woman. When an offer came from a flight school in Colorado, Cornelia accepted despite her mother's misgivings. She moved to Fort Collins and got to work as the only woman instructor in a government-sponsored pilot training program there. Before long she had another offer to work as a flight instructor, at a school where she would have more hours, more students, and more time in the air. And she'd still be part of America's push to prepare for a possible war by training men who might be needed as pilots. She didn't hesitate. In September, Cornelia boarded a ship for Hawaii and the kind of opportunity she'd dreamed of.[26]

• • •

Shortly after sunup on that December morning in 1941, Cornelia met her regular Sunday-morning student for his lesson. He would solo soon, and she had him take the small plane up and down several times to hone his takeoff and landing skills. Then, before heading back to the airport, she told him to fly a bit higher.

The student was at the controls and handling the plane well when Cornelia spotted a military airplane heading in their direction—not too unusual, since the civilian airport was right next to the military base at Pearl Harbor. That's where the US Pacific fleet of a hundred ships and other watercraft was based. It was also home base for nearly four hundred military planes. On a normal Sunday morning, though, military planes weren't typically in the air. Something didn't feel right about this particular plane.

> I jerked the controls away from my student and
> jammed the throttle wide open to pull above the
> oncoming plane. . . . He passed so close under us
> that our celluloid windows rattled violently, and I
> looked down to see what kind of plane it was. . . . The
> painted red balls on the tops of the wings shone
> brightly in the sun. I looked again with complete
> and utter disbelief.

Cornelia recognized those red balls as the emblem of the rising sun—the symbol on the Japanese flag.

I looked quickly at Pearl Harbor, and my spine tingled when I saw billowing black smoke. Still I thought . . . it might be some kind of coincidence. . . . For surely, dear God . . .

Then I . . . saw formations of silver bombers riding in. I saw something detach itself from a plane and come glistening down. My eyes followed it . . . and . . . my heart turned over convulsively when the bomb exploded in the middle of the Harbor.[27]

Bullets hit another civilian plane just behind Cornelia as she sped toward the landing strip. Once on the ground, she and her student ran for the safety of the hangar. She tried to tell her fellow pilots—all men—that the Japanese had attacked, but they only laughed. "I was damn good and mad that they didn't believe me," she said later. Just then a mechanic raced in and announced, "That strafing plane . . . killed Bob Tyce." Tyce, the airport manager and Cornelia's friend, was dead, and Cornelia's announcement was no longer a joke.[28]

Japanese forces had attacked the United States. Over thirty-five hundred American military personnel were dead or wounded. Battleships, cruisers, and destroyers had been sunk or badly damaged. And over three quarters of the four hundred American military aircraft at Pearl Harbor had been damaged or destroyed. It would take time to assess the disaster, and most Americans wouldn't hear what had happened for at least a few hours. But Cornelia knew right then that her country was at war.

The next morning, Fort went back to the plane she'd been flying, found it full of bullet holes, and suddenly understood how close she'd come to being killed. She realized that her family back in Tennessee had to be worried about her, but she had no way to tell them she was okay. Only military cables were going out of Hawaii for the time being. All she could do was wait and worry about her family worrying about her.

In Washington, DC, the next day, Franklin Roosevelt spoke to a joint session of Congress.

> Yesterday, December 7, 1941—a date which will
> live in infamy—the United States of America was
> suddenly and deliberately attacked by naval and air
> forces of the Empire of Japan.

By "a date which will live in infamy" Roosevelt meant no one would ever forget the evil done on December 7, 1941. Relations between Japan and the United States had been strained during the 1930s as Japan took over land in China and Southeast Asia. In 1940, Japan had joined Germany and Italy in the Axis alliance and the tension increased. By late 1941 the American military was aware of the threat of a Japanese attack somewhere in the Pacific. Any attack would be terrible. But Japan chose to begin its attack without warning at a time and place sure to result in the greatest possible damage and loss of American lives. Other attacks followed.

September 11, 2001

The Japanese bombing of Pearl Harbor was the deadliest attack ever made on American soil until September 11, 2001. On that day terrorists hijacked four US passenger planes and used them as weapons of mass destruction. They crashed the planes into the two towers of the World Trade Center in New York City and the Pentagon in Arlington, Virginia. The last plane crashed into a field in Pennsylvania after its passengers fought successfully to keep the terrorists from hitting their target— thought to be the Capitol in Washington, DC. The attack resulted in nearly three thousand deaths (just under twenty-five hundred people died in the attack on Pearl Harbor).

Americans had reacted to the attack on Pearl Harbor with shock, grief, anger, and fear of further attacks. They also felt strong determination to defend the United States and its values. Americans sixty years later reacted to the attacks of 9/11 in very similar ways. And just as people who were alive in 1941 never forgot the attack on Pearl Harbor, those living on 9/11 will remember that day for the rest of their lives.

Roosevelt told Congress about the American territories Japan had attacked in the hours after Pearl Harbor—Guam, the Philippines (an American territory at the time), Midway, and Wake Island. He admitted that the United States had never faced such a serious threat. Even so, his voice was calm and strong as he asked Congress for a declaration of war: "With confidence in our armed forces, with the unbounding determination of our people, we will gain the inevitable triumph."

Less than an hour later Congress voted almost unanimously to declare war on Japan.

Like Cornelia, Roosevelt had known as soon as he heard the terrible news from Hawaii that the United States was at war. But the nation faced more than a war against Japan. Because Japan was allied with Germany and Italy, FDR had to prepare Americans for a two-front war. They would be fighting Japan throughout the Pacific region and, at the same time, fighting Hitler's and Benito Mussolini's forces in Europe and North Africa. The task was enormous.

On Tuesday, December 9, as families like the Forts waited for news of their loved ones in Hawaii, millions of people gathered around radios at home or at neighbors' houses. Thousands more stood on sidewalks in front of stores that sold radios, or hovered in bars or restaurants. The president was going to speak, and Americans everywhere were desperate for news and reassurance.

Eight in ten adults across the country—just about everyone—listened to the president that evening. They were *terrified*. What if the Japanese kept attacking? Should they gather canned foods? Arm themselves? Send children away from the big cities and coastlines for their safety, as the British had done?

"My friends," Roosevelt began. This was the way he always started his fireside chats, as his informal radio talks were called. His voice alone calmed people. He told listeners to get maps of the world so they could follow along while he explained the attacks and the losses. Then he talked about enormous changes coming to American life. There would be shortages of all sorts of goods, he said, and rationing to make sure people all over the country had necessities. Every able man was needed in the military. "It will not only be a long war, it will be a hard war," he said. Roosevelt had trusted Americans to manage bad news during the Great Depression. Now he trusted them to manage even worse news. His words and tone assured people across the country that each of them could make a contribution.

> Every single man, woman, and child is a partner in the most tremendous undertaking of our American history. . . .
>
> The lives of our soldiers and sailors—the whole future of this Nation—depend upon the manner in which each and every one of us fulfills his obligation to our country. . . .
>
> We are going to win the war. . . .

Germany and Italy declared war on the United States just days later. Arguments about neutrality and isolation, the size of the military, the number of tanks or planes a factory could produce—all evaporated. Nearly everyone recognized that their country was at war, its very existence at stake. The United States suddenly needed the biggest military on Earth. The military needed more ships, tanks, and planes than all three Axis nations had yet produced or would ever produce. Recruiting, training, and equipping hundreds of thousands of men for such a military had to be done at lightning speed.

Despite Roosevelt's confidence, a nagging doubt hung in the air. The United States was now one of the Allied powers, and the Allies—Britain, France, China, and many others—were losing the war. Was it possible for America and its allies to defeat the Axis? One member of the Roosevelt administration said yes, the war could be won. But only "if this nation produces more and faster than any nation has ever produced before."[29]

The first step was to build powerful armed forces. Congress had moved to increase the number of men in uniform soon after the war had started in Europe, but far more soldiers, sailors, and marines were still needed. There were just under two million members of the US military at the time of the Pearl Harbor attack. A year later that number was nearly four million. By 1945 over twelve million Americans were in military service—

about 9 percent of the population. (Today less than 0.5 percent of Americans serve in the military.) But putting men in uniform was only a start. Wars aren't won with soldiers alone. Those soldiers needed weapons, food, clothing, shelter, and transportation. They needed trucks, tanks, planes, ships, and more.

The country scrambled to mobilize industry and civilians, in addition to the military. At first the nation pushed forward slowly, then faster and faster like the huge wheels of a locomotive. Roosevelt was right. Every person had a job to do in stoking the nation's engine and keeping it going.

The government asked farmers to plant bigger crops to feed the troops. Anyone with a yard was encouraged to start a so-called victory garden to grow some of their own food. Children helped with the gardens and pulled their wagons from house to house, collecting tin, rubber, and even cooking grease to be recycled into war materials.

The Kellogg Company stopped making cornflakes at some factories and started making K rations, the packaged food soldiers in the field relied on. A women's corset factory could use a lot of its technology and fabric to make grenade belts. A toy factory could manufacture compasses.[30] In Cornelia Fort's hometown of Nashville, Tennessee, a shoe factory started making combat boots, and a feed bag company retooled to make sandbags. It was the same everywhere. No one was going to be able to buy a new washing machine or lawn mower or bicycle for a very long time.

In 1941, American automobile plants had produced 3.5 mil-

The Great Migration

Over 90 percent of African Americans in the United States lived in the rural South in the early 1900s. Most were poor and lived with harsh segregation laws (known as Jim Crow laws) and frequent violence, including many lynchings, or hangings. During World War I industry grew in the cities of the North, Midwest, and West. Thousands of black families left the South to take jobs in those growing industries. This movement, or migration, of black families continued after the war when cotton crops across the South failed. Industry expanded again during World War II, and even more blacks left the South to find jobs. By 1970, when the Great Migration ended, over half of the nation's African American population lived outside the South.

lion cars. At the start of 1942, President Roosevelt issued an executive order—a power that presidents can use widely when the country is at war—ending automobile production completely. All the steel, rubber, and factory space were needed for military production. What about people looking for a new car or new tires? They were out of luck until the war was over.[31]

How fast could those automobile plants change their production? How many airplanes and tanks could they produce? How quickly?

General Motors started building tanks, trucks, airplane engines, and guns. Chrysler built fuselages (the part of a plane where people sit and cargo is stored). A Ford automobile at the time had about fifteen thousand parts, but a bomber needed well over a million. Yet Ford's Willow Run plant in Michigan geared up to send a new B-24 bomber off the assembly line every hour, twenty-four hours a day, with all million-plus parts in the right places.[32]

For the first time, industrial production in the United States went on all day and all night, with workers coming and going in three shifts. Americans were amazed at what their country could do in full gear, while the Axis nations—Italy, Germany, and Japan—were alarmed at the speed of American production. In Great Britain, Winston Churchill felt a sense of great relief to see the New World's "power and might" at work. Another British politician had told Churchill the United States was like "a gigantic boiler. Once the fire is lighted under it there is no limit to the power it can generate."[33] Apparently, that was true.

Millions of young men joined the military, many of them men who had worked in those all-important factories and mills. At the same time, factories and mills needed thousands more workers than ever before. Where would they come from?

Women in the Workforce

World War II changed the American workforce. As men joined the military and new factories opened to produce war goods, the need for workers grew. Poor women, especially minorities and immigrants, had been employed long before World War II. Their jobs were in textile factories, clothing factories, and food production plants, and as maids, cooks, and the like. Now women of all classes, married and unmarried, were encouraged to do their patriotic duty and go to work.

College-educated women were recruited to use their professional skills in military and government jobs. Thousands of working-class women took jobs at shipyards, in munitions plants, and on aircraft assembly lines. Those jobs paid far more than most traditional women's jobs, though women still made much less than men. This didn't change even when factory management discovered that, on average, women workers increased production while maintaining safety. In cities women worked as cabdrivers and bus drivers, maintenance workers, and mail carriers. In rural America they joined the Women's Land Army to do farmwork.

About six million women joined the workforce for the first time during World War II. The majority were married but did not have young children. Most middle-class married women remained at home but spent many hours in war-related volunteer work. All classes of working women, especially blacks, often faced resentment and discrimination in nontraditional jobs, though the government attempted to make their new roles acceptable to society. But most found their work a source of satisfaction and pride.

African Americans and members of other minorities had been unable to find work anywhere during the Great Depression, especially in the South. Once the war started, over three million black men went into the military, though most were restricted to support roles such as maintenance and cooking rather than combat units. Others found jobs in defense plants, factories, and ports. Soon thousands of black families moved from the Deep South to the cities of the North and West in a migration that changed the country forever.

Additionally, six million women of all backgrounds went to work, half of them for the first time.[34] Poor and minority women had always worked to help support their families. But most middle-class white Americans expected women to marry young, start a family, and stay in the home. Now women of all classes and races joined the workforce, many in jobs that women had never held before.

Many women took over positions on assembly lines and in heavy industry, work that only men had done before. Other women who had typing and bookkeeping skills went to work for the government or war-related businesses. Some carried their skills into the military once Congress made that possible.

In 1942, Congress passed laws allowing women to enlist in the military in limited and very specific roles. No women would be drafted. The navy accepted approximately 100,000 women in the enlisted and officer ranks of the WAVES (Women Accepted for Voluntary Emergency Service). They worked as secretaries, accountants, doctors (nurses served in a separate corps), engineers, and more—most on naval bases in the United States. They freed 100,000 men to serve on navy ships and in other combat jobs. Women joining the Women's Army Corps (WAC) enlisted as switchboard operators and bookkeepers. Other Wacs trained to be mechanics, bakers, and various support workers so that men who had been in those jobs could fight. Altogether, 150,000 women became Wacs and most served in the United States. Early in the war Wacs were paid less than men in similar assignments and received no retirement pay or insurance. But before the war ended, Wacs earned the same salaries and benefits as their army brothers and held the same ranks, and thousands went overseas to do noncombat military jobs. Some even died in the line of duty.

The army and navy had enlisted women in nurse corps since the early twentieth century. But during the 1930s those two corps had fewer than fifteen hundred members. Before the war was over, nearly sixty thousand women had enlisted in the Army Nurse Corps and another fourteen thousand served in the Navy Nurse Corps. They went wherever they were needed on land or on hospital ships that followed the fleets of destroyers and battleships. Many were wounded and awarded Purple Hearts. Others received Bronze or Silver Stars for their courage, and more than two hundred lost their lives in combat zones. Those women saved thousands of American soldiers' lives by getting aid to them quickly. Often they worked to save lives while shells exploded around them, and they protected their patients with their own

Military Medals and Honors

The United States armed forces awards medals to men and women who have shown extraordinary courage during military conflict. These medals include the following:

- the Congressional Medal of Honor—the highest military medal given, awarded for "gallantry and intrepidity at the risk of his life above and beyond the call of duty." As of 2017 only one woman had been awarded the Medal of Honor—Dr. Mary Edwards Walker, a civilian doctor during the Civil War (in 1917 the medal was restricted to military personnel).
- the Navy Cross, the Air Force Cross, and the army's Distinguished Service Cross—awarded for extraordinary heroism
- the Silver Star—awarded for gallantry in action
- the Bronze Star—awarded for heroic or meritorious achievement or service
- the Purple Heart—awarded to members of the armed forces of the United States killed or wounded while serving.[†]
- the Distinguished Flying Cross—awarded for extraordinary achievement or heroism "while participating in aerial flight."

bodies. They more than earned their medals and proved women's abilities and strength of character.[35]

• • •

Like the Waves, Wacs, and nurses, Cornelia Fort wanted to enlist. She'd seen the war up close before President Roosevelt even knew about the Pearl Harbor attack. But in January 1942 she and all the other civilian pilots were still stuck in Hawaii. The government had banned nonmilitary travel to and from the islands. Fort felt useless. "We wanted to return to the only thing we knew in the hope we could be of use to our country," she said.[36]

She wasn't alone. Most of the men trapped in Hawaii would be able to enlist with the Army Air Corps once they got back to the mainland. Would Cornelia be able to do that? Around the United States hundreds of women with pilot's licenses wondered the same thing and hoped to offer their skills. One woman wrote to an air corps recruiter,

> Isn't there anything a girl of 23 years can do . . .
> except to sit home and sew and become grey
> worrying? I learned to fly an airplane from a former
> World War ace . . . if I were only a man there would
> be a place for me.[37]

Nancy Love in the cockpit of the Queen Bee B-17, a heavy bomber. She and Betty Gillies were the first women to fly the B-17.

CHAPTER 4

Answering the Call

Cornelia Fort arrived in San Francisco from Hawaii aboard an ocean liner in March. She and the other civilian pilots on the ship knew they were taking a risk amid rumors that the Japanese would attack again, but decided it was a risk they had to take if they were to serve their country. Cornelia made a will before sailing, and once safely home, she wrote, "Nothing ever looked so beautiful to me as did the California shoreline as we approached it."[38]

Before she knew it, she was a celebrity of sorts. Reporters wanted interviews with the lady pilot who had been in the air when the Japanese attacked. What was it like? What would she do now?

"I want to get up in the air again," she told them. She didn't mention the telegram she'd received from Jacqueline Cochran a few months before the Pearl Harbor attack. Cochran had invited her to apply for the British ferrying service. The same telegram went to a number of women pilots with impressive flight records. Cornelia wasn't able to leave Hawaii and get to the East Coast in time to join Cochran, but maybe now . . .

Back at her home in Nashville, newspapers and magazines lined up to get her story, and schools asked her to speak. She told everyone who would listen that she and women like her could aid the war effort as pilots. "I wish I were a man—just for the duration [of the war]. I'd give anything to train to be a fighter."[39]

How could a woman think such a thing? Even though women might be nurses or do clerical work in the military, they didn't actually fight wars, and Cornelia knew she'd never fly in combat. Times were changing, but not *that* fast. (The military opened all jobs to women seventy-three years later, in 2015.) Yet she was disappointed to find only one war-related job for a woman pilot—teaching Civilian Pilot Training Program (CPTP) courses as she'd done in Colorado.

The CPTP had been training pilots since 1936. As tensions had mounted in Europe, and the United States had begun to build up its military, General Hap Arnold had proposed increasing the number of civilian men with basic piloting skills. Those pilots could transition to flying for the military very quickly if they were needed. Arnold knew that Germany had had such a program, and by the late 1930s its air force, the Luftwaffe, was formidable. When he presented his idea, President Roosevelt approved.

Civilian flight schools ran the program, usually at airfields close to college campuses, where students could take their ground courses. At first, women were allowed to make up 10 percent of each class, but that ended once the United States was at war and the need for combat pilots grew. Cornelia had enjoyed her time as a CPTP instructor before the war, but now she wanted more. Hadn't the women flying in the British Air Transport Auxiliary proved something? Surely, no one would argue that British women were more capable than American women. Besides, the American women pilots Jackie Cochran had recruited were doing just fine. And if women could teach men to fly planes, didn't it make sense that they could fly the planes themselves? Cornelia and other women wondered if anything would change the military's thinking.

No one wanted to say it out loud. The fact was, though, that by September 1942—nine months after the United Stated had entered the war—the Allies were losing. Even Franklin Roosevelt, always an optimist, called the news in the Pacific "all bad."[40]

Shortly after the attack at Pearl Harbor, the Allies faced defeat at Guam, the Gilbert Islands, Wake Island, Java, Singapore, and Hong Kong. Then Japan defeated American forces in the Philippines. The losses were horrifying. In May alone over 32,000 American men were killed, wounded, or captured. Of those casualties nearly 5,000 were members of the Army Air Forces, or AAF (restructuring in 1941 had made the Army Air Corps part of a larger organization—the Army Air Forces—with General Hap Arnold as its chief).

Victories at the Battle of the Coral Sea and the Battle of Midway in May and June of 1942 gave the country hope on the Pacific front, but the human cost of those victories, as well as the loss of planes and ships, was terrible. By the time the country had been at war a year, over 67,000 Americans—7,700 from the Army

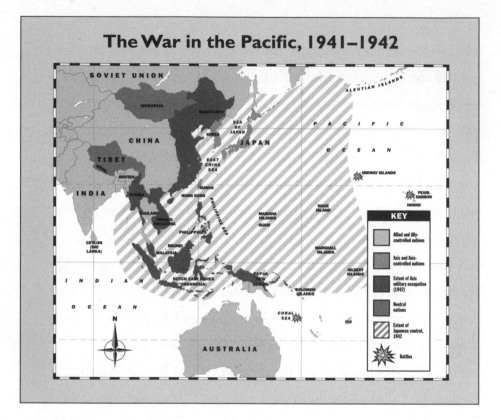

The War in the Pacific, 1941–1942

KEY

Allied and Ally-controlled nations

Axis and Axis-controlled nations

Extent of Axis military occupation (1942)

Neutral nations

Extent of Japanese control, 1942

Battles

Air Forces alone—had been killed, wounded, or captured.[41] Hap Arnold knew those numbers would get much worse before the Allies got the upper hand against the Axis.

Already many pilots had been pulled from the Ferrying Command—where they moved planes from factories to military bases—and transferred to combat to cover the numbers of men who had been lost. That left deliveries of new planes from plants to bases six weeks behind schedule. Aircraft coming off assembly lines now filled tarmacs, with hundreds and then thousands of planes awaiting delivery.[42] Something had to be done.

On September 1, First Lady Eleanor Roosevelt wrote in her daily newspaper column,

> There is just a chance that this is not a time when women should be patient. We are in a war and we need to fight it with all our ability and every weapon possible. Women pilots, in this particular case, are a weapon waiting to be used.[43]

Hap Arnold finally agreed. It was time to use women pilots in noncombat flying jobs.

Nancy Love, who had described her idea for using women to ferry military planes to the Army Air Corps planning division in 1940, now worked for Colonel William Tunner doing scheduling and routing for the Ferrying Command. Tunner was desperate for more pilots and believed Nancy when she told him there were excellent women pilots who could form a squadron very quickly. She had done the research and had a list of eighty-three highly qualified candidates—nearly every woman in the country who she thought could meet the program's requirements. Tunner asked for permission to pursue Love's plan and got the okay on September 5. Nancy Love would lead a women's squadron to be headquartered at New Castle Army Air Base in Delaware. There the women would learn the army's way of doing things and then begin flying military aircraft from factories to the bases where they were needed. Nancy started sending telegrams that night.

Cornelia Fort was near the top of Nancy Love's list of pilots to recruit, and one of the first to receive Love's telegram. If interested, Fort should report immediately to Wilmington, Delaware, for an interview and flight test. If accepted, she would start training right away. Cornelia didn't hesitate. She sent her mother a hurried telegram.

> The heavens have opened up and rained blessings
> on me. The army has decided to let women ferry
> ships and I'm going to be one of them.[44]

Also at the top of Nancy's list was Betty Huyler Gillies, who worked for an aircraft company on Long Island in New York and had known Love for some time. Not more than a dozen or so women in the country were licensed to fly the kinds of big ships she flew. Short and trim, Gillies looked younger than her thirty-four years, but the way she carried herself and her easy smile showed the confidence of a great pilot.

An original member and now president of the Ninety-Nines, the club to which Jacqueline Cochran, Nancy Love, and many other women pilots belonged, Betty had been urging women pilots to get ready for the chance to fly for their country. When Nancy Love's telegram arrived, however, she was torn. She'd mourned the tragedy at Pearl Harbor and wanted to help. But she and her husband, Bud, were already mourning another tragedy: Their youngest child, a daughter just four years old, had died of leukemia soon after the Japanese attack. Betty's grief ate at her night and day.

Betty and Nancy were friends, and Betty knew they'd work well together. Bud was an executive and test pilot with Grumman Aircraft—a company building military planes. His civilian job was considered essential to the war effort, so he wouldn't be called into the military and would be there for their two older children. And while focusing on ferrying military planes might help her through her grief, Betty worried about leaving her family. She asked Bud what he thought. He told her to go.

Gillies flew to Wilmington the next day and was the first woman to qualify for the program. Cornelia Fort was second in line. They were now members of the Women's Auxiliary Ferrying Squadron (WAFS).

Love's plan was to find the nation's most experienced women pilots, give them four or five weeks of transition training on military planes and procedures, and start ferrying backlogged aircraft as soon as possible. She insisted the women have at least five hundred hours of flight time, though men entering military transition training needed only three hundred hours. Only about a hundred American women had that kind of experience, and twenty-five of them were already with Jackie Cochran in England. Some had husbands fighting overseas and no one else to care for their young children. Others were already working in war-related jobs. Twenty-eight women came to Delaware at their own expense in response to Love's telegrams and passed their interviews, physicals, and flight tests. They were the best of the best, averaging twelve hundred hours of flight time when they volunteered.

Most of these recruits, including Betty and Cornelia, were college educated and well off, which made sense because taking flying lessons and owning or renting a plane cost a lot more than most people had during the Great Depression. And several of the "originals," as they later called themselves, were beyond well off. Phyllis Burchfield's family owned oil wells in Pennsylvania. Barbara Donahue came from the Woolworth five-and-dime store empire.[45]

Those who were not so well off had had to scramble to learn to fly, washing airplanes or doing mechanical work in exchange for lessons. Some flew for a living—one as a stunt pilot, another as a barnstormer. And several taught in the Civilian Pilot Training Program. Stunt pilots, barnstormers, and CPTP instructors sacrificed their higher wages to be ferry pilots. They would make $250 a month, less than they'd been making before and just two thirds of what civilian men ferrying military planes made. These women didn't question their lower pay—women almost always made less than men for the same work. Besides, this was the first opportunity to actually fly for their country.

Love was confident that four weeks of twelve-hour days would get her pilots ready to fly a variety of military aircraft, complete paperwork, and follow army regulations. Still, there was no time to waste.

The women assumed Congress would pass legislation militarizing the WAFS before long. But getting anything through

Congress took time, and ferry pilots were needed immediately, so Love had agreed to keep the program civilian in order to get started right away. And though she knew women could do the job, the military considered the program only experimental and wanted time to assess it before asking Congress to act.

That left some questions unanswered as the first volunteers gathered at New Castle: Did women need the same kind of fitness training as men who might go into combat? Should they follow the rules of military discipline? Wear uniforms? Be treated like officers? Salute? It was more important to get right to work than wait for all the answers.

Betty Gillies, Cornelia Fort, and the rest of the women hauled their luggage across planks over a muddy path to the wood building that was to be their home at New Castle. They settled into tiny rooms with iron cots, thin mattresses, and no curtains or shades on the windows, which overlooked a military base with hundreds of men walking past day and night. The women would have to turn off the lights or step into the hall to get dressed and undressed.

Because they were civilians, the women had to pay for their transportation to New Castle and for their own housing and food. But because they were on a military base and doing what looked like military work, they were told to be ready for regular military inspections of their rooms.[46] Men who worked as civilian ferrying pilots didn't have inspections. Neither did officers in the military, and all military pilots were officers. These women had careers, marriages, children, and homes of their own. Room inspections? If that's what the army wanted, then fine.

Ground courses were the same for all the women pilots and some of the volunteers resented having to take courses they'd actually taught as instructors. Barbara Poole of New Jersey, for example, had been the youngest commercial pilot in the country at seventeen. When she was a CPTP instructor, every student she taught passed all the government tests to get a license. Yet now she had to take those same courses as if she'd never seen the material before. Evelyn Sharp, from a poor Nebraska family, not only taught flying, but had over three thousand flight hours and was a barnstormer, demonstrating skills many pilots only dreamed of.[47] She, too, had to start from scratch.

Even as a young child, Cornelia Fort had hated being told what to do. At New Castle she argued, "As flight instructors, we know all that."[48] Nancy Love pointed out that not all the women had been instructors, and she wanted everyone to stick together no matter what. Even Cornelia stopped arguing. It wasn't easy, though, especially when the women realized their courses were longer and more detailed than the same courses men in transition training took.[49] Why couldn't men and women all take the same courses together? And why did the military think women needed more classroom time than less experienced men?

The same frustrations followed the women into the cockpit.

At first the WAFS pilots were restricted to practicing takeoffs and landings in tiny PT-19 trainer planes, though they were all already licensed to fly much bigger aircraft. Most of their instructors were very good. They recognized how skilled these trainees were and sympathized with their frustration. But a few didn't like the idea of women flying military planes. When Gertrude Meserve, a flight instructor at Harvard and MIT, showed her logbook to her check pilot—the instructor who gives a pilot his or her final test or check flight to determine if the pilot "checks out" on a particular type of plane—he seemed not to believe that her total of two thousand hours in the air was accurate. "I can always tell once I see how a girl flies whether or not she has padded her logbook," he said sarcastically.[50] Gertrude hadn't padded her logbook at all. She was happy to prove it at the controls of the aircraft, almost daring the check pilot to find fault with her skills. He didn't.

Eventually the women started flying bigger ships, which posed challenges for Betty Gillies. Betty had flown a lot of big aircraft, and she had far more experience than her instructors. Her skills were not the problem; her size was. She joked that it was a good thing she had signed up so early. Once all the requirements were in place, she would have been turned down for being too short. Military aircraft had no adjustable seats or controls, and at just under five feet two inches, Betty couldn't reach the pedals in the big military planes. But being short wasn't going to stop her.

She had a pair of wood blocks made to fit over the foot-controlled rudder pedals.[51] It was like she'd grown three inches taller. Other petite pilots used their parachutes as seat cushions or brought pillows into the cockpit so they could see over the instrument panel (similar to a car's dashboard). However, wood blocks and pillows didn't help when a woman was too short to swing herself onto an airplane's wing and into the cockpit. Instead a woman like Gillies asked a ground crewman to give her a lift— an actual lift—so she could climb into the aircraft.

As long as they could do what they'd signed up for, they'd find a way to make it work.

Not long before they finished training, the women at New Castle learned they were going to have to march in review with actual military units. They couldn't believe that they lacked the benefits of being part of the military but still had to march like soldiers. And they didn't see what marching had to do with flying.

At first they ran into problems—and one another. Literally. Though one or two of them had done a little drilling in high school, most had no experience, and they hadn't been assigned a military drill instructor to help them. Nancy Love was supposed to lead her troop, but she had never marched, didn't know the commands, and had a very soft voice.

One day the women drilled on an old, unused runway, unaware that the pavement ended in a steep drop-off ahead of them. When the first row of the formation reached the edge, they stopped short, though Nancy hadn't ordered them to. The second row bumped into the first, and the third into the second, and then the whole group was piling up like a flock of sheep at the top of a cliff. When Nancy, who'd been thinking about other things, finally noticed, she forgot any proper commands and yelled, "Stop!" not sounding at all military. The women didn't look or sound very military either as they collapsed on the ground laughing.[52]

Despite their difficulties, the WAFS pilots didn't stop practicing. Determined not to embarrass themselves or the program, they kept at it, with Betty Gillies using her limited experience to help.

The Army Air Forces had issued the women standard, though oversize, flight coveralls and goggles as soon as they arrived at New Castle. But now the formal, or dress, uniforms Nancy had had designed arrived. Military pilots got a $250 uniform allowance; the civilian women didn't, so they paid for the uniforms themselves. By then their marching looked quite military, and the uniforms made them feel official, even important. The women of the WAFS were ready to take off and do what they'd dreamed of doing.

Cornelia Fort wrote,

> I think the most concrete moment of happiness came at our first review. . . . Suddenly and for the first time we felt a part of something larger. . . . We were marching with the men, marching with all the freedom-loving people in the world.
>
> . . . A bomber took off, followed by four pursuit planes. We knew the bomber was headed across the ocean. . . . I could hardly see them for the tears in my eyes.[53]

Avenger Field near Sweetwater, Texas, where the WASP held its training program after moving from Houston, Texas.

CHAPTER 5

Becoming Wasps

J ackie Cochran returned from England to work out the details of her plan for women pilots just a few days after Nancy Love started recruiting pilots for the WAFS. Cochran's plan was more complex and ambitious than Love's, but that was no surprise—Jackie's plans were almost always bigger than anyone else's.

Cochran wanted to train women who had limited experience as pilots, as well as use highly experienced flyers. She also wanted her recruits to do various kinds of military flying in addition to ferrying planes from factories to bases. By opening the program to hundreds or even thousands of women with only some flying experience, the Army Air Forces could free hundreds or thousands of men for combat missions. In addition to ferrying, women could fly target-practice planes, test new or repaired planes, and more. Like Love, Cochran agreed to keep her program civilian and experimental so the training could get under way quickly.

Hap Arnold approved the plan. Jacqueline Cochran would

lead the WFTD—the Women's Flying Training Detachment, headquartered in Houston, Texas.

Soon thousands of applications poured in. Before the war was over, more than 25,000 women had applied. Only a fraction ultimately made the cut, with 1,074 successfully completing training. Trainees had to be smart, hardworking, skilled, and physically fit—like the men. But they were also expected to behave at all times in a proper and ladylike way. Love and Cochran knew their programs would draw attention. Everything the women pilots did would be examined and scrutinized. The women could very well appear on the cover of a weekly magazine like *Life*, read by millions of Americans. Sure enough, as soon as the press learned of the WAFS, magazine and film crews clamored for interviews with the women at New Castle. If the public or military leaders or Congress thought even one woman was creating a scandal, the whole experiment could be shut down. These pilots had to prove that women were serious, mature, and professional, on top of being skilled.

Cochran's school in Texas was just down the road from Ellington Field, where thousands of men trained as combat pilots. The women trained with civilian instructors at a civilian airfield on the edge of Houston Municipal, a civilian airport. Houston was a much smaller city in 1942 than it is today. There were no barracks available as the program began, and finding a place for the women to live was difficult. Most of the WFTD trainees rented rooms with families who had extra space, or stayed at inexpensive motels. They weren't allowed to use the airfield's dining room, and training started so early each morning they couldn't buy breakfast in town. They went without.

At first the flight school's classrooms weren't available for the women's program either, because a men's CPTP program was still under way. The women's training program would have to make do until the men were finished and gone. Even the bathrooms at the school were off-limits to Cochran's trainees, and the women had to walk a half mile to the nearest toilet. Worse, some of their flight instructors didn't want to train women and said so—loudly.

The women of the WFTD came from diverse backgrounds and included a Hollywood stuntwoman and a nurse who reached her rural patients on horseback.[54] The first class in Houston included several young women who'd never been away from home before. Some had argued with their parents about volunteering and had to convince them they wouldn't become "loose women" out on their own. Others were college students who'd started flying with the Civilian Pilot Training Program. And some were married, with careers, and husbands fighting overseas. Like the women in Delaware, they'd all paid their own way, some even selling their belongings to do it. Others were well off and could afford to fly just for fun. But no one was quite like trainee Marion Florsheim.

Red-haired Marion, a very wealthy woman who chose to stay in the nicest hotel she could find, had learned to fly so she could chauffeur her prizewinning Afghan hounds to kennel club

The Tuskegee Airmen

African American men were not allowed to serve as military pilots until 1941. In that year a flight training center was established at a school for blacks in Alabama—Tuskegee Institute. The African American men who trained there as fighter pilots, crewmen, maintenance workers, and other support staff became known as the Tuskegee Airmen. Their achievements during World War II proved that black air and ground crews were the equals of white crews. Their success helped pave the way for a fully integrated military in 1948.

competitions around the country. She arrived in Houston with trunks of designer clothing and two enormous red-haired dogs that wore bows on their heads to match her traveling outfit.[55] Though Florsheim stood out against ranchers, teachers, and secretaries, she knew how to fly and wanted to serve her country, just like the other women. That's all that mattered.

The trainees may have been a diverse group when it came to

wealth, education, hometowns, and the kinds of lives they led. But with the exception of two Chinese American women and one Native American, all were white.

The US military was segregated in 1942 and remained segregated throughout the war. Black and white men served in different units and often in different jobs, with blacks usually limited to low-level support work. The Army Air Forces had started accepting African Americans for flight training only a few months before the women's program started, and they were in black squadrons and groups.

Some men in the top ranks of the military and government simply believed that African Americans had inferior abilities. Others knew blacks were perfectly capable of doing the same jobs whites did, but they worried about the turmoil that integration of the military would create. A majority of Americans, military and civilian, had grown up with segregation and lived largely segregated lives. Most whites resisted any change to the way things were. Many generals thought that integrating the military would cause resentment, hostility, and distrust among soldiers and sailors. Any lack of cohesion, or unity, could mean disaster on the battlefield and was a risk the generals and the president would not take.

Jackie Cochran had the same concern as those generals. She turned down any black women who applied to the program regardless of their qualifications. She said of one impressive young woman, "I had no prejudice whatever with respect to the color or race of my candidates but . . . the complication she had brought up . . . might . . .

Rocking the Boat

Cohesion—the ability of a group to stick together—is a major concern for the military. Soldiers, sailors, flight crews, and others must be able to rely on one another in difficult circumstances. They must trust one another with their lives. And they must share a deep commitment to achieving the group's goals. Anything that threatens that cohesion is a serious problem. In the 1940s the issue was racial integration of the military. In more recent years the questions of LGBTQ in the military and women in combat have been hotly debated. In 1948 the military was integrated. In 2011 bans on gays serving in the military were lifted. In 2015 women were accepted into all military jobs, including combat positions. In each case people inside and outside the military predicted that the change would destroy cohesion and readiness. Discrimination, harassment, and resentment did present problems in some areas after 1948, 2011, and 2015—and in some areas still do. But studies have found that overall cohesion and readiness in the armed forces has remained strong, and the majority of military men and women support the changes that have been made.

be the straw that broke the camel's back" of the program's success.

Accepting black women pilots certainly would have made the WFTD program different from the military.[56] And Jackie Cochran and Nancy Love were already pushing their luck when it came to gender. Was Cochran correct in thinking integration would have threatened the success of the WFTD? There's no way to know for certain. What is certain is that her program—just like the Army Air Forces—failed to recruit some very highly qualified pilots, men and women.

•   •   •

Most of Cochran's trainees in Houston had less flying experience and training than the women in Delaware. So while their program was similar, their classroom courses were longer and more detailed. They memorized army flying procedures, practiced Morse code for radio communication, and learned enough mechanics to take an engine apart and put it back together. They studied navigation techniques to find their way across the country alone and without radar, and meteorology so they could assess the weather as they flew. The men down the road at Ellington Field covered all the same material in their classes. But one WFTD instructor insisted on giving the women an arithmetic test before they got started, something the men didn't take. That instructor wasn't sure the women could "do any of this stuff."[57] They could.

They could also fly the worn-out, rickety, bucket-of-bolts planes they'd been assigned. The twenty-two planes were all different types of trainers, and the women's instructors admitted they'd never flown some of the models themselves. The men training nearby had better planes to work with, and even CPTP classes on college campuses boasted better fleets.[58]

Cochran considered the planes unacceptable, and her determination and stubbornness paid off. She soon found better trainers for the program—reliable primary trainers, or PT-19s. With one roofless cockpit in front and one in back, the trainees flew with their instructors behind them talking through a tube attached to their helmets. Unfortunately, some instructors yelled angrily at every move instead of talking—

African American Women in Aviation

Women who wanted to become pilots in the 1920s and 1930s faced barriers men did not. Black women faced double barriers; even at schools that accepted women, they were barred from flying lessons because they were black. Bessie Coleman was the first African American and Native American woman to earn a pilot's license. When she couldn't train to be a pilot in the United States, she saved

her money, learned to speak French, and went to flight school in France. She got her license in 1921 and returned to the United States, where she became famous as a stunt pilot. Coleman dreamed of opening a flight school for blacks but died in a plane crash at the age of thirty-four before she could fulfill her dream. Other black women followed in Coleman's footsteps. In 1938, Willa Brown became the first black woman to earn a pilot's license in the United States.

leaving their students ready to scream in frustration. The instructors had controls so they could override a student's mistakes when talking through the tube wasn't enough. They used the controls less and less as the student grew more proficient and finally soloed.

Then there was physical training, or PT. Jumping jacks and running to build stamina. Neck exercises to avoid whiplash. Push-ups and pull-ups for upper body strength. The trainees were perpetually aching, sore, and sweaty, but in the end PT paid off.

After WFTD graduation Betty Jane Williams worked testing newly repaired planes. It was a dangerous assignment, since a missed or poor repair could mean disaster. She took a ship up one day and put it into a spin—a standard part of testing. This plane, though, wouldn't come out of its spin. Betty Jane spiraled downward, her concern turning to real fear as she tried everything she could think of with no luck. Finally she decided she had to bail out and let the plane crash, as terrifying as that was with almost no parachute training. Then she realized she couldn't bail. The force of the spin—centrifugal force—was so strong she couldn't move her hand far enough to reach the hatch.

"As they say, my life passed in front of my eyes," she recalled. Split seconds felt like hours before an instructor's words popped into her head: *If the plane won't reset, put both hands on the stick and "pretend that you're whipping a big bowl of mashed potatoes and go clear around. Sweep the cockpit."* Betty Jane grabbed the stick and forced it in a circle against the terrific force, using every ounce of strength she had. Those pull-ups may have been the thing to save her life as the plane straightened out just five hundred feet above the ground.[59]

PT included marching, too, and the women in Houston hated it as much as the women in Delaware did. At least building upper body strength had an obvious purpose. But marching? They were saved by a young lieutenant assigned to a nearby supply depot who saw the women going to and from the terminal in an unorganized mass. At first he didn't know who they were or why they were there. They certainly didn't look military.

The women had been wearing their civilian clothes for training, since the army hadn't issued them flying gear yet. They'd discovered that ordinary women's clothing wore out quickly in flight training and they needed to replace things. However, women's slacks were rare in 1943 and none were sold in Houston, so the women bought men's pants and tried to make them fit. They'd become a ragtag-looking bunch.

The lieutenant was curious, and once he found out about the WFTD program, he volunteered to help. Lieutenant Alfred Fleishman understood the point of marching. Competent drill would boost everyone's morale and make them feel more military.[60] He explained that to the trainees and gave them clear instructions and support, spending hours teaching them to march and leading them in calisthenics. Soon their attitude toward drill improved and they gained confidence.

Eventually the army sent flying gear for the trainees, and they could put away their street clothes. As civilians, however, the women would not be issued uniforms. They were happy to have the sturdy coveralls for flying, but they admitted the new gear didn't boost their pride or sense of dignity. The coveralls were leftovers from men's training classes—large men, at that.

Marie Muccie of New Jersey was just five two, shorter than the required five feet four inches, but she had so impressed Jackie Cochran in her interview that an exception was made.[61] Marie's khaki coveralls would have fit a man a foot taller and a hundred pounds heavier than she was. She had to roll the sleeves and legs over and over, making them bulky and heavy. Then she found a belt to cinch at her waist, leaving gallons of fabric billowing over the top. Without the belt, the pants' crotch was at her knees and she had to walk like a penguin. Nothing could fix the armholes, which drooped practically to her hips.

She and the other petite women had to laugh at what they called their "zoot suits"—named for the baggy-legged, high-waisted, big-jacketed men's suits popular with jazz musicians at the time. They joked that the suits came in "all sizes—large, Large, and LARGE."[62] At least all the extra material might help keep them warm in an open cockpit. But they didn't have access to washing machines, so they'd been doing their laundry in their bathroom sinks, and the coveralls were too big to fit in a sink. The women ended up wearing the zoot suits into the shower and soaping and rinsing them there.

Lieutenant Fleishman couldn't do anything about the size of the zoot suits, but he helped the trainees with more than marching. He believed in the WFTD program. When a new group of women arrived for training in February 1943, he told them they were "part of an experiment which will do more to advance the cause of equality for women than anything that has been done so far."[63]

In the fog, rain, and mud of the Houston airfield, he taught the women how to survive the army. "There is a simple directive about Army life," he said. "'If the Army can dish it out, I can take it.'" Fleishman told them how important that attitude was. "If . . . it should develop that women can't take it," he said, "it might affect the whole program. . . . You will have to stick out your chin and show them."[64]

By then the military's need for more pilots was clear, and Cochran was asked to double the number of women in her training school. Changes had to be made. The WAFS and WFTD were combined and became the Women Airforce Service Pilots (WASP). Cochran would continue to run the training center in Texas, and Love would stay with the ferrying squadron in Delaware.

The training center was moved four hundred miles northwest from Houston to Avenger Field in Sweetwater, Texas. And while applicants to the training school still had to have a pilot's license, the flight time requirement was reduced from seventy-five to thirty-five hours (men entering the same training needed no pilot's license and no flight time at all). The Wasps remained civilians, though they still expected that eventually Congress would militarize them like other women's auxiliaries. But the trainees were working too hard to think much about it.

On the day the Houston pilots transferred their trainer planes from the old field to the new, residents of Sweetwater took picnics and went to watch. Some made bets about how many planes being piloted by women would crash, bets no one made about planes piloted by men. Those betting against the women were disappointed. A hundred planes left Houston, and a hundred planes landed smoothly at Avenger Field.[65]

Ann Baumgartner had been accepted for WASP training in January 1943. She'd meant it when she promised to help the war effort as she returned from England to the United States in 1939. She'd found a job with a medical research company in New Jersey and hoped to connect her premed education with the war effort. One afternoon Ann went to the roof of her office building to get some fresh air and saw a plane come through the clouds and across the Manhattan skyline. *"Imagine . . . looking at the world stretching away around you,"* she thought. She would learn to fly.

"I had read about the . . . women pilots in England," she said, and later remembered thinking, *"I just might be able to join them if I could fly an air ambulance."*[66]

Ann took a trial flight and knew immediately she was made to be a pilot.[67] Several months later she got her license and started working toward the two hundred hours needed for a commercial license. She was close to that two hundred hours in September 1942 when she read Eleanor Roosevelt's column supporting the use of women pilots in the war effort. Then she learned about the Army Air Forces' plan for such a program. She was soon on her way to Avenger Field in Sweetwater.

At the time, Sweetwater was known for its rattlesnakes, tarantulas, black widows, and scorpions, as well as constant dusty wind and temperatures over one hundred degrees a good part of the year. In 1943, Sweetwater also became known as the home of the only all-women air base ever.[68]

Ann settled into a barracks close to the training center, which was more convenient than the living arrangements in Houston, though not terribly comfortable. The women wrote home about "chewing dust" and "Texas dust in their teeth."[69] Roommates took turns throwing telephone books at the two-inch-long roaches that ate holes in their robes and slippers. They learned to check their boots for scorpions before putting them on each morning. But most didn't think to check their pant legs, until one trainee was stung as she got dressed. In a lot of pain and frightened at being poisoned, she went to the emergency room. She was "lucky," the nurse told her. Sweetwater's scorpions had poisonous and non-poisonous seasons. Her sting was only miserable, not deadly. Yet she felt stung again when she got back and found her bunkmate charging the other trainees a dime to see the attacker, now trapped in a glass jar.[70]

Locusts descended on the training center too. They worked their way under sheets, got into women's hair, and were so thick on the runway, planes skidded on them as they landed.[71]

On some nights the intense Texas heat kept everyone from sleeping in the stifling barracks, so the women took their small cots into the yard between buildings to find a breeze. Some of them also found a rattlesnake or two curled up with them when they woke. Others got up covered in crickets. The choice between sleeping with critters or sleeping in unbearable heat was a tough one.

There was another entirely different kind of pest to deal with at Avenger as well. A surprisingly large number of military pilots had "engine trouble" near Avenger and asked permission to make emergency landings—more than a hundred in the first two weeks after the Wasps arrived. The sudden rash of problems turned out to have nothing to do with engines and everything to do with the flyboys, as military pilots were often called. These men simply wanted to see the women pilots up close. Jackie Cochran made it clear that only true emergencies should result in unscheduled landings. It was irresponsible to report fake emergencies.

No one suggested that because a few men flying for the military were irresponsible, all military pilots were irresponsible. Such a suggestion would be unfair. Cochran recognized, though, that attitudes were different for her women. Fair or not, one bad apple was very likely to spoil the whole program.

Even after interviewing every applicant carefully, both Cochran and Love put rules in place to make sure their programs' reputations were safe—rules that men did not have at all. In Sweetwater each barracks had a housemother, the way college dorms at the time did. The women weren't allowed to smoke in town, though men and many women smoked everywhere at the time (people didn't know yet that cigarettes cause cancer and other diseases). Trainees were told to dress modestly and nicely when off base and not to socialize too much. Aside from a few eye rolls, the women generally went along. The stakes were high and their focus was on graduating and getting into the sky. But Avenger Field was soon known as Cochran's Convent.[72]

• • •

The program was extremely demanding, and not every woman who started WASP training finished. Some had family emergencies or chose to quit. That was the one advantage of being civilians—the women could resign if they wanted to. Unfortunately, some washed out, meaning they failed and were forced to leave, everyone's biggest fear.

Overall, the women's washout rate was about one third, the same as men in military pilot training.[73] But a few classes had far more than the average number of failures. In one case twice the average number of trainees washed out, and the women suspected they were being judged differently from the men. Ann Baumgartner wrote, "It seemed as though we were judged on the very way we walked, moved, and thought."[74]

It was possible that some check pilots wanted to be combat pilots, resented their assignments, and took their frustration out on the WASP trainees. It was also possible that a few check pilots were embarrassed to see women flying as well as they could. "Why the heck do [they] have to be afraid of us?" complained one Wasp.[75] A few women felt some sympathy for them, since "one day they were supermen and all of a sudden the next day the girls were doing it."[76]

Regardless of the reasons, it became obvious that a small number of instructors failed women unfairly. Both men and women in pilot training found washing out devastating. But for a woman to wash out knowing she was as good as anyone else was too much.

And when at least one woman with excellent skills suspected she washed out because she wouldn't let her instructor kiss her, it was time to do something.

A review board appointed to investigate confirmed the women's suspicions. Some check pilots were intentionally targeting women for failure or getting back at the women who refused to date them. (Today this kind of behavior is called sexual harassment and, in the workplace, is cause for being fired.) The board made changes so trainees who failed with one instructor could train for a short time with another instructor before being washed out. That slowed unearned failures from instructors like Captain Maytag. He'd gotten his nickname from the popular washing machine because he washed out so many Wasps.[77] He might not have faced punishment for his behavior, but if he was angry about not flying combat missions, he would have to find another way to show it.

Long hours, hard work, lots of studying, sore muscles, and a common love of flying built bonds among the women. Many made friendships that lasted the rest of their lives. When each pilot soloed for the first time, the others dunked her in the wishing well—a twenty-foot-wide, round, shallow pool where pilots often tossed coins for good luck. The women passed the time spent waiting for the weather to clear or a plane to be ready by playing cards. And, like regular military units, they made up new lyrics for familiar songs they could march to.

"The Battle Hymn of the Republic" became "We Were Only Foolin'" and started, "When we go to ground school we're as happy as can be." Other songs included "Yankee Doodle Pilots" and "Zoot Suits and Parachutes." A college fight song turned into "Buckle Down, Fifinella." The songs' lyrics were funny and spirited and, sometimes, a bit rude. The Wasps loved them. The earliest classes started a WASP newspaper with articles about flying, movie reviews, and war news. Other classes kept it up. And once the people of Sweetwater got used to the idea of women trainees at Avenger, they invited them into their homes for Sunday dinner and welcomed them to the town pool in the blistering summer heat.

Most Wasps thought Avenger Field was the most desolate place they'd ever seen when they first arrived. Later they realized that they'd miss seeing Fifinella greet them each time they returned to Avenger.

Many official army units had mascots—cartoon figures of some sort that informally identified and were said to take care of the unit. The Wasps weren't military, but they, too, had a mascot—Fifinella. Fifinella was a female gremlin created by Roald Dahl in his first children's book, *The Gremlins*. Dahl had joined the British Royal Air Force in 1939 as World War II began. He knew the tales British airmen told about impish creatures who played tricks and sabotaged their planes. Dahl started writing stories about gremlins and fifinellas (female gremlins) as he recovered from serious injuries after his plane crashed in the Sahara. When his stories were published, Walt Disney suggested an animated film based on *The Gremlins*. The film was never made, but Disney did release the story as a book with illustrations by an animator at Walt Disney Studios. Those illustrations included drawings of Fifinella, or Fifi.

The Wasps asked Disney for permission to use Fifi as their mascot. Disney, who had developed mascots for many military units, agreed. The women thought of Fifi as nice rather than naughty, a protector of sorts. She welcomed everyone who entered Avenger Field with a smile on her goggled face. Class after class of women—eighteen classes in all—smiled back. Despite the hard work, discomforts, and fatigue, the Wasps at bases all over the country had reason to smile. As Betty Jane Williams explained, "The ability to do something you love and to do it at a time of need for your country–nothing is better than that if you have much patriotic blood in your system."[78]

Ann Baumgartner and her classmates certainly felt that way when they walked across the stage at their graduation at Avenger Field. Jacqueline Cochran gave each of them silver wings, wings she had designed and paid for herself, since the military wouldn't provide them to the nonmilitary WASP. These women were ready. According to one graduate, they all had "the love of flying, of patriotism, and also the spirit of adventure."[79] Like all the women who finished training and graduated as Wasps, they would need those traits when they got to their assigned bases and started their real work.

Ferrying pilots Cornelia Fort, Evelyn Sharp, and BJ Erickson sit on the wing of a BT-13 with Barbara Towne and Bernice Batten standing. Fort, seated on the left, was killed less than two weeks after the picture was taken.

CHAPTER 6

Ferrying for Uncle Sam

★

The Allies began to make progress against the Axis early in 1943. Russia stopped the Germans in eastern Europe that February. In May, British and American forces defeated the German army in North Africa and moved to invade Italy. The Allies also got the upper hand against German U-boats in the Atlantic, allowing supply and troop ships to sail more safely to England. In the Pacific, Americans and Australians battled the Japanese on island after island in miserable, bug-infested humidity. But victories in places like Guadalcanal meant they could advance toward Japan itself.

The US Army Air Forces spent 1943 attacking Germany from the air with American B-17 bombers flying from England across France and over Germany. The German air force—the Luftwaffe—fought back ferociously, and hundreds of Allied planes and crews were lost. Eventually American industries developed new kinds of engines and fuel systems—technology that allowed American and British fighter planes to escort the

Allied Progress in Europe, 1943–1944

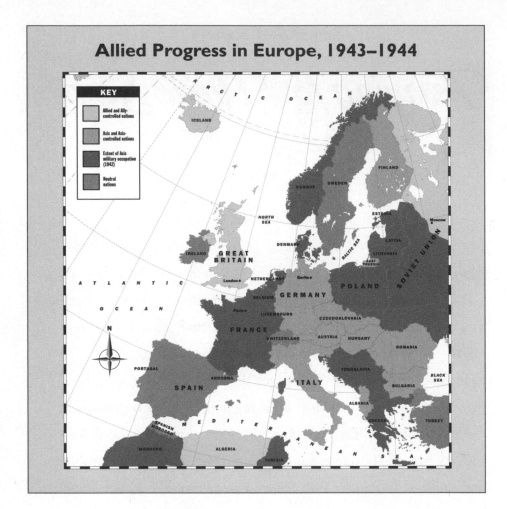

bombers over more miles without stopping. Fighter, or pursuit, aircraft were fast and maneuverable. Their mission in Europe was to protect the slower, heavier bombers from German defenses. Once fighter planes were able to escort bombers all the way to Berlin, the Allies gained control of the air. That, in turn, would eventually allow Allied soldiers to reach Germany and end the war.

Those fighter planes were crucial, and most people thought of fighter pilots the way they had thought of the aces of World War I—manly, daring, brave, skilled, and usually very handsome. It was true that fighter pilots needed tremendous skill, quick reflexes, and nerve. Fighter pilots risked their lives every time they took off, and thousands died in aerial combat. Of course, thousands of military men on ships and on the ground risked and lost their lives too. But somehow, flying fighter planes seemed more dashing, perhaps more glamorous, than any other military job. Even other pilots thought so.

If flying fighters was the job every military pilot wanted, ferrying planes from factories to bases was the job none of them wanted. Pilots who ferried planes in the United States flew long hours from factory to military base, base to maintenance plant, maintenance plant to base. Over and over. Often tedious and lonely, often uncomfortable, never glamorous but terribly important. When a regular AAF pilot trained to fly a bomber or fighter plane or cargo plane, that's the only craft he flew. He became an expert on one particular aircraft and might fly nothing else for a very long time. On the other hand, ferrying pilots often flew a particular type of aircraft only once or twice. Instead of becoming experts on one plane, they had to be able to fly any kind of plane, from a single-engine, open-cockpit trainer to a four-engine B-29 Superfortress bomber—all on a moment's notice. It wasn't unusual for ferrying pilots to keep the instruction manual for an unfamiliar plane on their laps while they flew. They had no chance to become experts on a particular plane, and that was dangerous. Each type of aircraft had a different feel, different quirks, and a different level of power. It responded differently to turbulence or wind. It took off and landed differently. But the ferrying pilots flew all types of planes, and many pilots found the constant change unnerving.

As undesirable as ferrying was, though, the Wasps were happy to take ferrying jobs—the more the better. It was a contribution to the war effort and a challenge they welcomed. By the time they left training in either Delaware or Texas, they could fly primary, basic, and advanced trainer planes. They added to their credentials every chance they got, some pilots setting their sights on flying everything the Army Air Forces had. Before the war ended, Wasps had flown seventy-eight different kinds of aircraft. That's an average of fourteen different types of planes per Wasp, more types of planes than a pilot in any other job was ever likely to fly.[80]

The women were assigned to bases all over the country, from Long Beach, California, to Onslow County, North Carolina, and from Fort Myers, Florida, to Detroit, Michigan. The commanders at many of those bases welcomed them as equals. Others made it very clear they didn't want women pilots anywhere near them, though eventually half the ferrying pilots in the United States were women. Male or female, ferrying pilots never knew from one day to the next where they'd go, what kind of plane they'd fly, or how long they'd be gone.

Barbara Jane Erickson recalled a marathon ferrying adventure when she "made four transcontinental flights in a little over five days."[81] She gave credit to the weather, the quality of her four planes, and some luck. That may have been too humble. Not many pilots could handle eight thousand miles in such a short time, flying the kinds of planes BJ Erickson was piloting.

Teresa James—who started flying to impress a boyfriend and then fell in love with planes instead of the boy—learned the hard way to be prepared for anything. One morning she was assigned to fly a P-47 Thunderbolt pursuit plane from New York to Indiana. She figured she'd probably fly another P-47 back to New York later in the day. Teresa delivered the first plane and got some lunch, expecting to be in New York with the second plane by late afternoon. But the operations officer in Indiana said he needed a pilot to take a P-47 to California. James agreed. She hadn't packed to be away overnight, but a quick trip to the PX for a toothbrush would get her by as long as she didn't spill anything on her shirt at dinner. In Long Beach, California, the next day an operations officer asked if she knew how to fly a P-51 Mustang. She didn't, but it was a beauty of a one-seater fighter. The officer handed her an information pamphlet and told her she was flying the Mustang to Florida in the morning.

Teresa rinsed out her shirt and underwear before she went to bed. In the morning, after practicing a few takeoffs and landings in the P-51, she was on her way. However, bad weather forced her to land and stay in Texas for several days—rinsing her clothes every night, since the base didn't sell women's things. On some mornings her undies were still damp; she couldn't wash her pants at all—they'd never dry overnight.

James finally got the P-51 to Fort Myers, Florida, only to find orders to take an AT-6, a trainer plane, to Oklahoma. For days she'd been eating dry sandwiches from base snack bars along her routes because she hadn't brought her uniform jacket with her and wasn't allowed in an officers' club without it. When she ran into another Wasp delivering a plane in Tulsa, she borrowed the woman's jacket so she could get a real meal. Then she took a P-39 Airacobra, yet another fighter, to Montana and immediately had orders for another flight. This time she nearly fell over in relief: She was to take a P-47 to New Castle, Delaware. Home at last.

Still wearing the washed-out shirt and undies and the baggy, saggy, filthy pants, Teresa James returned to Delaware—four weeks, six planes, seventeen states, and eleven thousand miles after she'd left for a day flight.[82] Her sister pilots met her in the barracks and practically collapsed laughing at the way she looked. The women quickly learned to squeeze a few toiletries, a skirt, blouse, and shoes for a ground trip back to base, and some clean underwear, into a small duffel they could cram into any plane. There wasn't room for anything more.

Ferrying pilots often made unscheduled landings because of bad weather or mechanical problems. At bases where no one had met a Wasp, the women sometimes ran into issues that the men who ferried planes did not.

Thousands of P-51 Mustangs like the one Teresa James flew were being sent to England as quickly as they came off the assembly lines to fill the RAF's desperate need for them. At 430 miles per hour, the Mustang was faster and more agile than any plane yet built and drew everyone's attention. Nancy Love wanted the women to fly the new fighters, and they did—sometimes with surprising results. Pilot Carol Fillmore got orders to take a P-51 from California to New Jersey. She was near Athens, Georgia, when dusk forced her to find a place to put down. Fillmore called the Athens control tower and asked for permission to land. Silence. She tried again. Nothing. By then Carol was circling the field and called once more. An angry controller radioed back for her to "stay off the air, we're trying to bring in a P-51." Fillmore couldn't see any other Mustangs in the air and finally realized what had happened. "For your information," she told the tower, "the lady who is on the air is in the P-51." With that she made her final approach toward the runway as the controller said, "You're fine, you're coming in fine, just great." The dozens of trainees who had come outside to see the big ship they all wanted to fly watched Carol open the canopy. One trainee yelled, "It's a girl!" Carol Fillmore climbed onto the Mustang's wing to a huge ovation.[83]

Barbara Poole was ferrying a PT-19 a long distance when bad weather forced her to make an unscheduled landing. The little trainer plane had no radio, so she watched carefully and landed without clearance. Before she knew it, a high-ranking officer was ordering her away from the plane and off the base. She tried to explain, but he wouldn't believe she was a ferrying pilot. Even when she got Nancy Love on the phone, he didn't believe it. Barbara had no choice—she went into town to find a hotel and a place to eat. The officer had told her, "Don't come back!" So how was she going to get her plane and take off when the weather cleared? She didn't want to end up in jail, but she needed to deliver that plane on schedule. As soon as the sky began to brighten the next morning, Poole hurried back to the base, sneaked onto the tarmac (bases were less secure then than they are today), and took off without looking back.[84]

Early on, military command had concerns about women ferrying planes, and they kept close watch on the WASP's delivery statistics. Could women deliver planes safely and on time as well as men? One mission answered this question.

More than twenty PT-17 open-cockpit Stearman biplanes were headed from Montana to Tennessee. The ferrying team assigned to them included six women, with Teresa James as team leader for the whole group. In that kind of operation, individual pilots set their own pace, and they don't fly in formation because it's safer to be farther apart and on their own. The planes took off from Montana one right after the other, each pilot deciding where to refuel and spend the night. But though all the planes left Montana at about the same time, they didn't all land in Jackson, Tennessee, at the same time or even on the same day. The first six PT-17s to reach their destination were piloted by the six women on the team. Two days later nearly a dozen planes had still not arrived.

Air Transport Command wasn't at all happy with a delivery rate of just over 50 percent safe and on time. Those planes were needed. Radio reports indicated that some of the missing pilots had gotten lost and two planes had been damaged. And the rest? Apparently those pilots had decided to take detours to visit girlfriends or family and have a little relaxation time.[85]

When the higher-ups saw which pilots had landed first they realized that the women's delivery rate was perfect. Air Transport Command's concerns about the competence of women ferrying pilots rightly evaporated.

Ferrying planes was nothing like combat, and no one pretended otherwise. But ferrying had its own risks. Jeanne Robertson was in a group ferrying planes over Texas when a sudden storm swallowed the group whole. Unable to go over or under the bad weather, Jeanne looked frantically for a place to land and saw an airfield. Ground crewmen ran to meet her as she taxied toward a hangar. They grabbed the wings of her small plane to hold it against the high wind the storm had brought. Another pilot landed behind her, and others found landing strips elsewhere. Sadly, "one fellow tried to continue on in spite of the storm," Jeanne said. "He disappeared. We wondered if he tried to go through the storm and his plane was torn apart, but nobody ever knew." They did know they were lucky to have landed safely.[86]

In March 1943, Cornelia Fort—witness to Pearl Harbor and a WAFS original—wrote to tell her mother about the used but slick gray convertible with red leather seats she had just bought. "If anything should happen to me—which I don't think will—I want Louise [her sister] to have the car," she said.

Less than two weeks later she and several male pilots at Long Beach were assigned a ferrying mission taking BT-13s, basic trainers, to Dallas. After refueling in Midland, Texas, Cornelia got ready to take off again. Some of the men who had landed at about the same time asked if she'd like to practice flying in formation with them on the way to Dallas. That was against the rules for ferrying pilots, but the terrain they were crossing was open and empty, and it seemed like the perfect place to hone their skills and have some fun. Cornelia should have said no, but she'd always been a bit of a daredevil. Whatever her reason, she agreed.

There had been cases of inexperienced male pilots showing off for the women by flying very close to their planes or rolling above them—a good reason not to fly in formation. It's possible that's what happened in the sky over Texas, though there was no proof of such negligence. But midway to their destination one of the pilots saw two planes veer off course. One wavered and then recovered. Horrified, he watched the other little plane, Cornelia's, start a slow spin and then roll and dive nose-first right into the ground. He had no doubt he'd witnessed a pilot's violent death.

Investigators concluded that Cornelia had made no mistakes. The BT-13 flying beside her had come too close, and its landing gear had struck her wing, tearing off the tip and much of the wing's edge and propelling the jagged metal into the body of the plane. Fort had probably died instantly when the other plane struck, they said. She'd had no chance to bail out.[87]

For Nancy Love, Betty Gillies, and the other originals, the news was a terrible blow—like losing a family member. The twenty-four-year-old who may have been the first witness to the attack at Pearl Harbor now became the first woman pilot in American history to be killed while flying for the military.

Military pilots killed while flying were buried with full military honors, and their families received insurance money. As a civilian, Fort was not eligible for military burial or honors. Fortunately, Cornelia's family could afford to bring her remains home to Nashville and honor her with a formal funeral. Hundreds of people attended the service, including Nancy Love and BJ Erickson. They were pleased when the stone marker at her grave was inscribed, KILLED IN THE SERVICE OF HER COUNTRY. But the Fort family was not allowed to drape Cornelia's casket with an American flag as at a military funeral. They could not honor her the way the families of military men and women honored their loved ones.

Most people who had family members in the military during World War II hung small banners in their front windows with a blue star for each family member serving in the armed forces. If one of those family members died, a gold star replaced the blue. As the war went on, gold stars in windows blanketed the country, each one symbolizing a tragedy and honoring a hero. The Forts had not hung a blue star for Cornelia. And now her mother could not hang a gold-star banner in her window, though she had lost a child to the war just as if Cornelia had been in the military and been killed in action.

Cornelia's sister pilots mourned her death, and many resented the fact that she didn't receive military recognition. Those who had reported to Delaware with her felt their loss keenly. They knew it could have been any of them. But none of the women resigned or lost their nerve to fly. When a base in Michigan restricted their women pilots to flying nothing bigger than primary trainers soon after Fort's death, the women were furious. The government's official report on the tragic accident stated clearly that there was no pilot error on Cornelia's part. Even if there had been, why would it affect other women pilots? If the male pilot involved in the accident had died, no one would consider restrictions for every male pilot.

Less than a month later Betty Gillies and three other originals were assigned to take Canadian trainer planes from Maryland to Calgary, Alberta, Canada—more than twenty-five hundred miles. Rather than think about Cornelia's death, they made their trip a tribute to her.

Betty challenged the group to fly the fairly slow little planes (PT-19s averaged 100 miles per hour) from the first light of day to the last with as few stops as possible. The four landed, checked into a motel to sleep a few hours, and set off again as soon as the sky was light. They repeated that pattern the following day and the next. Gillies wanted to demonstrate the Wasps' determination and skill. She wanted to show what the women pilots were made of.

When the four women safely delivered the trainers to Calgary in just four days, they set a record for the trip.[88] They saw the commendation they received as a commendation for all the women flying for the AAF, especially their friend Cornelia.

The women flew on, fully aware of the dangers, and fully aware that their risks were small compared with those of the pilots overseas. The inconveniences they faced were small in comparison too. But some of those inconveniences applied *only* to women ferrying pilots and not to men doing the same job.

Men in the ferrying service sometimes faced dirty looks or insults because they weren't in combat. The women certainly didn't experience the same kind of prejudice, but when the men delivered their planes to the assigned base, they usually got a ride back to their home base on another plane headed that way. Top brass didn't think the women should hitch rides with male pilots without a chaperone, so the Wasps had to find a train or bus or civilian flight back to base. It was slow and inconvenient, but that was the rule.

As the Wasps waited in train stations or airports, people sometimes mistook them for nurses or Wacs or Waves. When they learned who they really were, some told the women they had no business doing men's work in the military. Others thanked them for their service as pilots and made room on train benches for an exhausted woman pilot to sleep. Those gestures were welcome comfort.

On many bases the women ferrying pilots weren't allowed to eat in the officers' club, though all military pilots were officers. When a commanding officer said no, they had two choices: argue their way into the dining room, or find a ride into town and pay for a meal in a restaurant. At one base the commanding officer refused to give the women housing or meals, even when they were stationed there for months.[89]

The women put up with the inequalities and occasional insults because they loved their jobs and had the respect of many military men. Moreover, they knew that every time one of them ferried a plane from factory to base, it was one more plane on its way to combat overseas. That plane would help win the war. Sometimes the women left notes in the cockpits wishing the combat pilot who eventually sat there good luck. On at least one occasion a combat pilot sent a thank-you note back. All the insults in the world wouldn't change these women's feelings about what they were doing.

Not long before she died, Cornelia Fort wrote,

As long as our planes flew overhead, the skies of America were free and that's what all of us everywhere are fighting for. And that we, in a very small way, are being allowed to help keep that sky free is the most beautiful thing I've ever known.[90]

Wasps at Camp Davis in North Carolina flew many kinds of missions, often piloting planes in serious need of maintenance.

CHAPTER 7

Yes to Every Job

★

Ann Baumgartner—who had heard the start of the war at her uncle's home in England—took off into the bright sky over Camp Davis in North Carolina in a B-34 twin-engine bomber. She flew out over the ocean and turned parallel to the shoreline, towing behind her what she described as a "ragged cloth sleeve" somewhat like the advertising banners small planes tow over crowded beaches. Gunfire erupted and Ann saw strange "round blobs of smoke outside the window." She realized the gunners below weren't doing too well. They were supposed to fire their live ammunition at the cloth sleeve and then count the bullet holes in the fabric later. But either they were very bad shots or they didn't understand their instructions. Those young men were shooting at the cockpit where Ann sat. Still, they were trainees, new to firing at airplanes, and they needed to learn.[91] Blanks would have been less nerve-racking for Ann, of course, but blanks didn't fire exactly like the real thing, so they could throw off a soldier's aim in a real battle. Live ammunition was the only way to learn.

Ann hadn't felt anything hit her plane, so she turned and flew in the opposite direction, still parallel to the shore. More gunfire. More blobs of smoke. As long as she didn't think too much about the live ammo or the possibility of German U-boats lurking under the waters of the Atlantic, it was a beautiful day for a flight along the beach.

Target towing was one of the jobs Jacqueline Cochran had in mind when she proposed her training program. It required skilled pilots with steady nerves, and she was certain her women could do it. They worked in three- or four-hour shifts and often landed to find their planes riddled with bullet holes. The job was an odd combination of very boring and very scary, especially with newer gunners. However, it was training that would enable those men to bring down enemy aircraft before they could attack other Americans or allies. Even so, it took a toll on the tow pilots.

WASP Kaddy Steele, a small-town girl from northern Michigan who had learned to fly with the CPTP, reported that tow target pilots had to realize there were "always human errors, there was a definite margin of error, especially in the low-altitude missions . . . because [the gunners] would sometimes get over-exuberant. But there were incidents where the airplanes were shot and . . . shot down."[92] The women were willing to take the risk. After all, combat pilots had to fly over enemy gunners doing their best to shoot them down. And as Kaddy said, "I knew that never again in my lifetime would I get an opportunity to fly those airplanes."[93] She'd take the risk.

Jackie Cochran hoped the Wasps would do all the flying military pilots did, with the exception of combat. The women in the program agreed and enthusiastically accepted every assignment that came their way. While they took pride in being able to provide what the army needed, they also did it for the good of the group. "We didn't want to say no to any job," Betty Jane Williams said. If they refused risky jobs, military men might think it was only because they were women. "So we did a lot of things that we knew were dangerous," she went on. "We did them to keep the program rolling and keep up our image."[94]

At night Wasps took planes up and flew in big ovals, higher and then lower and then somewhere in between, while men training in artillery worked to keep them in their searchlights. The Wasps had learned instrument flying skills by working with a machine that simulated night flying. Once they'd mastered the machine, they practiced in real planes with hoods over their heads so they could see nothing but the plane's instruments even in daylight. That training and practice served them well in searchlight flying. Any pilot who made the mistake of looking out the window into the searchlights would be temporarily blinded and likely to feel dizzy, so everyone flying searchlight training shifts relied on instruments for the entire four hours they were in the air.[95]

Other Wasps learned to tow the gliders the army used for delivering supplies and men behind enemy lines. A glider—a craft without an engine—made no noise, and that silence increased the odds of landing safely in enemy territory. The gliders were big enough to carry pallets of food, ammunition, or medical supplies and could also carry troops and even military vehicles like jeeps.[96] A tow from a powerful motorized plane got the gliders into the air, and then they were on their own, with the pilot guiding and landing them using only the power of aerodynamics. Flying a glider was very different from flying a motorized plane. Every glider pilot required special training and practice. That's where the Wasps came in—they flew the motorized planes, usually C-60 cargo planes, that towed the gliders into the air for training.

Taking off in a huge C-60 while towing two gliders was a real challenge. The C-60 was twice the size of most fighter or trainer planes and big enough to carry three tons of cargo.[97] The plane's size made it slow lifting off the ground even without gliders attached. The gliders made it slower. Once up, the C-60 tow pilots had to keep their planes low, the way pilots would overseas to stay under the enemy's radar. They were told to stay below "the height of a windmill."[98] That left little room to maneuver or make adjustments. And the sudden loss of weight when the gliders were released could force the C-60 up and out of control if a pilot wasn't prepared. It was difficult, dangerous work, but the Wasps found it a thrill to watch the gliders move silently and smoothly away across the sky.

In addition to target and glider towing, the Wasps worked as flight instructors, teaching ground courses and flying classes for military pilot trainees—classes many Wasps had taught with the CPTP before the war. They also provided air taxi service for military bigwigs and played the part of the enemy for military pilots learning to maneuver and fire in a dogfight. Some were assigned to "attack" men in training, spraying them with tear gas or flying low and fast over them as if they were firing on them. A handful of the most skilled Wasps even flew in a top secret experiment.

Most people today would probably guess that drones (motorized planes guided remotely instead of by a pilot in the cockpit) are a fairly new invention. But drones first appeared during World War I, and when World War II began just over twenty years later, drones were still in the experimental stage and far less sophisticated than the drones of the early twenty-first century. Engineers hoped to use drones to deliver bombs without risking crews' lives. They thought drones might also be a better way to train antiaircraft gunners than target towing. They kept their plans secret, and so did the men and women involved in the testing.

Modern military drones can be directed by a pilot thousands of miles from the drone itself, but the drones of World War II had to be controlled by a pilot in close radio range. That pilot directed the drone with radio signals, a lot like directing a remote-control car or model airplane. Beeping sounds from the unmanned drone plane told the pilot what to do. The so-called beep pilot sat in a plane called the mother ship, which followed the drone. Wasps often piloted those mother ships, with the military beep pilots sitting next to them directing the drone.

Drones were expensive to make, and the military couldn't afford to lose one because an inexperienced beep pilot made a mistake. So during training a third pilot sat inside the drone at a set of controls. That safety pilot was supposed to touch the controls only if the drone was about to crash. Then he or she could take over and save the drone, similar to the way a flight instructor could override a trainee's error.

The little PQ-8 drones looked like Walt Disney planes—short, chubby, and red, with a turned-up nose. They were cute, but they weren't designed to hold a human pilot and were very uncomfortable. Safety pilots had to be agile enough to squash themselves into the drones. They had to be very skilled, so they could recognize what every pitch or turn or bump of the little red plane meant. And they had to have enough self-discipline to keep their hands off the controls unless there was a true emergency. Just four pilots in the entire drone program were trained for the difficult work of the safety pilot. Two were Wasps, including Lois Hollingsworth, whose degree in engineering and aeronautics gave her a clear advantage over most flyers.

Hollingsworth admitted that trying to concentrate in the cramped space wasn't easy, and every sudden move of the drone made a safety pilot want to grab the controls. She forced herself not to. As she explained, "We were supposed to delay taking over until the very last minute, otherwise the beep pilots would never know how good they were."[99]

• • •

As stressful as Lois's job could be, there was another flying assignment that many veteran pilots—civilian or military—dreaded or even refused. Every time a plane went in for repairs, it had to be tested before going back into service. The AAF's mechanics knew how serious the smallest flaw could be at 400 miles per hour, but there weren't nearly enough mechanics or spare parts to take care of all the planes that needed work. Mechanics sometimes overlooked problems or postponed repairs. The test pilots, some of them civilian pilots and some military pilots who were back in the United States after months of combat missions overseas, were there to find out if a plane really needed repair and if a supposedly repaired plane had actually been fixed.

WASP Gene Shaffer had grown up close to Oakland, California, where she loved watching small planes near her home. She was in high school there when Amelia Earhart landed at a nearby airfield after flying solo from Hawaii to the West Coast in 1935. Shaffer worked on her high school newspaper and managed to talk her way into the hangar where Earhart was giving a press conference. She could hardly believe she was standing right next to one of the most famous women in the world and was surrounded by reporters from nationally known newspapers. She asked Earhart what advice she had for high school students. "Aviation is the career of the future," the tall, soft-spoken woman told her.[100] Shaffer believed it. Six years later she had earned a pilot's license and was looking for ways to use it in the war effort.

Now a WASP at Gardner Field in California, Shaffer found

herself testing planes she knew no pilot in his or her right mind would take up, since pilots could and did die because of mechanical failures. In fact, that may have been what killed Amelia Earhart. Even so, someone had to find out if seemingly minor damage was a reason to ground a plane or not. The Army Air Forces didn't want to risk military pilots who could be used overseas, so Wasps were welcomed. "We were expendable," Shaffer said. She knew the risks but became an experienced test pilot. On one occasion she was testing a training plane and needed to find out if the wing was secure: "I . . . remember the rivets popping off."[101] She landed safely and went on with her work.

Shaffer knew what she did was dangerous, and she knew some men who worked as civilian pilots for the military tried to avoid maintenance test flights. But the stress of the job hit home when she flew with an experienced combat pilot. Shaffer recalled,

> There was this fellow who came back from England with fifty [combat] missions to his name and an "I'm a pilot . . . I've been to war" attitude. Well, they put him with me. . . . We went up there and did a spin [a standard part of testing]. We got into the spin and it wouldn't come out. . . . He said, "You take it." So I did all the normal things you do; I tried everything, but it wouldn't come out. . . . I put the power in and wiggled the stick . . . and it finally caught . . . and I thought, Whooh![102]

Shaffer never saw that combat pilot again. He was ghostly pale when they landed, and he went straight to the maintenance officer to ask for a new assignment.[103] Shaffer kept testing planes.

The maintenance problem was particularly severe at Camp Davis in North Carolina. Trainees at Camp Davis—over forty thousand men at any one time—were there to learn how to use antiaircraft guns of all kinds. The hundreds of pilots assigned to Camp Davis were there to be the "enemy" the trainees fired on. About fifty of those pilots were Wasps.

Camp Davis wasn't a popular assignment location to begin with. The base was surrounded by swampland, and the weather was often hot and always humid. Insects swarmed around everyone's hair and buzzed at their ears. Barely visible flying pests flew into mouths and up noses. And the mosquitoes were famous for attacking like a squadron of fighters. With fewer than a hundred women and nearly fifty thousand men on the base, unwanted attention from *human* pests was also a constant hazard.

Wasps at Camp Davis did target towing and searchlight flying, as they did at other bases. At Davis, however, they ran into two very serious problems. One officer described both issues at once when he said, "These planes are dispensable [easy to replace] and you're dispensable."[104]

Many of the planes used to tow target sleeves were redlined, meaning they had lots of broken pieces and shouldn't be flown. But Camp Davis was so desperate for aircraft that if a plane could get off the ground it was used regularly, redlined or not. The women flew those unreliable planes day after day as if they were in fine condition. Instruments sometimes worked and sometimes didn't, so a pilot couldn't rely on the readings. Tires were worn thin, since most new tires went to Europe for planes in combat. Those thin, worn tires frequently blew out as a plane landed. As many as five planes a day had blowouts at Camp Davis. Engines quit in midflight—two in one day in late August 1943. Radios didn't work either. The list went on and on. Pilots were told to fill out a Form One sheet to describe any mechanical problems they experienced in flight. But the mechanics admitted there was no point in filling out those forms because there weren't any parts to fix anything.[105]

Maintenance at Camp Davis couldn't have been much worse. And the attitude of the commander and many enlisted men there didn't help. Before the women even arrived some mechanics and others mumbled threats of a strike if they had to "serve any powder puff pilots."[106] Others asked to be transferred rather than work with women. And the camp commander had restricted the Wasps to flying tiny Piper Cubs—single-engine, two-seat planes that weighed less than a thousand pounds—though the women had checked out on much bigger planes.

Jacqueline Cochran was furious. Some commanders of ferrying groups had limited the women at their bases to flying small planes six months earlier. They had soon gotten orders from General Tunner (he had been promoted in June 1943) to use the same standards for the women as they did for men. Those orders didn't apply to the commander at Camp Davis, since he wasn't leading a ferrying group. But it made no sense to do things differently there.

When Camp Davis's medical officer insisted on monthly physical exams for the women, Jackie Cochran flew down and demanded an explanation.[107] Men didn't have monthly exams and neither did women at other bases, she pointed out. Some men, including some male doctors, believed women's menstrual cycles had a negative effect on their physical and emotional state and that they couldn't manage difficult tasks during menstruation. Such thinking may have been the reason for the medical officer's decision, though the head of medicine for the AAF had ordered his officers to leave the issue of menstruation up to the women individually. By the time Jackie left Camp Davis, the monthly physicals had been canceled.

Marion Hanrahan had fallen in love with flying as a child. She even cut classes in high school to hang around an airfield and beg for rides and flight time. She later admitted having to go to different airports on different days to stay ahead of the truant officer— the official responsible for making sure students were attending school—who was trying to chase her down. At twenty-one she became a WASP and was assigned to Camp Davis.

All her time at airfields turned out to be a very good thing for Marion. In addition to the mechanics course she had taken at Avenger Field, she knew quite a bit from working in hangars in exchange for lessons. After she had two tires blow and one engine fail in a very short time, Marion realized she was piloting "flying jalopies" and took matters into her own hands. She got to know the mechanics, saw how overworked they were, and helped them in her spare time. Then, when she was assigned a flight, she talked to them about the particular plane so she'd know what to expect. Other Wasps followed her example.[108]

No matter what the pilots did to protect themselves, though, Camp Davis was a dangerous place for pilots. In the first weeks there "I think we lost three men and four women," Marion recalled later.[109] She never got over Mabel Rawlinson's death.

Mabel had grown up the middle of seven children on a small farm in the red clay of rural Virginia. Lean and freckled, she looked like a girl who spent a lot of time outdoors and knew how to put in a day of hard work. Mabel was a good student, and when she finished high school, she moved to Michigan, where she lived with an aunt and worked her way through college. After gradua-tion she worked at the Kalamazoo Public Library, heard about the CPTP program, and learned to fly. She joined the WASP as soon as she found out about the program.

One evening at Camp Davis, Mabel and several other pilots, including Marion Hanrahan, were assigned to do a check flight to test their night-flying skills. When Marion commented that she hadn't had dinner yet, Mabel offered to switch times with her so she could eat. Mabel and an instructor climbed into an

A-24, a small two-seat bomber, with Mabel at the controls and the instructor behind her in the gunner's seat.

Nearly all the A-24s at Camp Davis had problems, and this one was no different. But the items listed on the Form One sheet didn't involve the engine, so up they went. Everything looked routine until Mabel prepared to land. Witnesses reported seeing the plane bump the treetops as it approached the runway. Someone else thought he saw flames. The instructor later reported,

> I felt the throttle moving back and forth and
> realized the engine was dead. . . . I took over and
> told the student to jump. I then shouted at the
> student to jump. . . . Somehow I knew she hadn't.[110]

The plane crashed, splitting in two between the cockpits, and the dreaded siren started screaming the news of an accident. Marion Hanrahan said,

> We were in the dining room when we heard the
> siren that indicated a crash. When we ran out on
> the field we saw the front of her plane engulfed
> in fire, and could hear Mabel screaming. It was a
> nightmare.[111]

Rescue workers and others raced toward the flames and smoke. The swampy undergrowth and vine-covered trees slowed them down. When the terrible screams stopped, they knew it was too late. Mabel Rawlinson was dead.

Marion knew it would have been her in that A-24 if Mabel hadn't offered to switch places. Why hadn't she bailed out, or climbed out on the ground? A quick investigation showed that one of the items listed on the Form One sheet was a broken latch on the front hatch. It wouldn't open from the inside and had not been fixed. Mabel hadn't gotten out of the plane before the flames reached her because she couldn't.

Shaken by the horror of what they had witnessed, Rawlinson's fellow Wasps collected money to send her body home for burial. They knew her family couldn't afford to do it, and regulations didn't allow for burial money, since Wasps were still civilians. Altogether, thirty-eight women died flying for the AAF. All thirty-eight times a fellow Wasp went with her sister pilot's body to tell the family what had happened. BJ Erickson said, "I had to go six times and tell their mothers that their daughters weren't coming home, and I was only twenty-two." She was especially bothered by having to tell those mothers that their daughters would have no military honors, not even a flag.[112] Mabel's friends and family ignored part of the rule. They bought a flag for her casket. Mabel had died for her country just as any military pilot might have, and they weren't going to deny her a flag.[113]

For days the Wasps at Camp Davis couldn't focus on anything but what had happened to their smiling friend. A friend who'd loved books and singing and flying. They thought about why she had died. Maintenance. If the hatch had worked properly, Mabel might have survived as her instructor did.

Just a month later Betty Taylor Wood—married only six weeks earlier—was killed at Camp Davis in another A-24. She was chauffeuring an army chaplain that day, and when she started her landing, something didn't feel right. She pulled up and accelerated in order to go around and make a second approach, as she'd been trained. That wasn't an unusual thing to do. It was like a driver backing up and readjusting to pull into a parking space. However, before Wood's plane climbed into the air again, it suddenly rolled and crashed onto its back, crushing Betty and her passenger.

Fellow pilot Kay Menges had recently reported a sticky throttle on that same plane. She felt sick. Nothing ever got fixed, and a sticky throttle could cause that kind of accident. Yet there were other possibilities too. No official report was ever made, but the women heard unofficially that Jackie Cochran, who had come to Camp Davis after Rawlinson's death and again when Wood died, found sugar in the gas tank of Betty's plane.[114] Sugar was a surefire way to stall an engine, and it meant sabotage. If there really was sugar in the gas tank, someone had put it there on purpose.

The Wasps at Camp Davis had endured constant harassment. Now, with two deaths in a month and not a trustworthy plane on base, morale fell to rock bottom. Marion Hanrahan and another pilot quit the program. For those who stayed, the laughter and singing the women usually shared were gone. Some of the pilots said they'd lost the nerve to fly. Others were losing weight because they were too jumpy to eat. Jackie Cochran talked with the women and concluded that there were more incidents of sexual discrimination, maintenance problems, and accidents among Wasps at Camp Davis than at any other base in the country.

Women at other bases sometimes experienced discrimination and resentment among the men they worked with. At bases where commanders welcomed and respected them, they were generally treated as equals. At Long Beach Army Air Field in California, for example, the women were seen as pilots with the skills to get desperately needed planes to their destinations. Nancy Love checked out on more than fifteen different kinds of airplanes in just a month at Long Beach—no one restricted her to small trainer planes because she was a woman. Eventually eighty women were assigned to ferrying duties at Long Beach and had nothing negative to say about the military pilots and commanders there. A report from Buckingham Army Air Field in Florida said that the ground and air crewmen had "grown to respect the blue WASP uniform and . . . admire the women who wore it."[115] The same was true at other bases. Why couldn't something be done about the situation at Camp Davis?

Cochran worried that if she made an official report to the AAF about the harassment at Camp Davis, it could put the whole WASP program in danger. If top military brass thought discrimination or, worse, sabotage was widespread, they might cancel the experiment. If they thought the women themselves were somehow inviting the resentment at Camp Davis, it would "prove" that women couldn't do the job. The program wouldn't end because the women were incompetent. It would end because too many men couldn't accept women as equals.

Cochran made no official report and kept any evidence she had secret. She wouldn't risk the whole program because of problems at one base. The women there would have to persevere.

As most of the women pressed on with their work, several of the men who had asked for transfers earlier had a change of heart. They might not have wanted to work with women pilots, but that didn't mean they wanted them dying. The men had actually gained respect for the skill they saw among the Wasps. As one enlisted man said, "We better stick around here and see these girls through." Moreover, the camp commander couldn't deny that officers overseeing artillery training had started asking for Wasps because they found them more reliable than the male pilots doing the same jobs.[116]

Like Betty Gillies and so many others, the Wasps of Camp Davis stuck out their chins and showed them they could take it. They were shaken, but they weren't defeated, and most continued to accept every job that came their way. Dora Dougherty explained their persistence: "The country was at war, submarines were seen at our coasts. We were all motivated to do whatever we could to further the effort for peace, for our country to win the war."[117]

A Wasp points to the sky on the wing of B-17 Miss Patricia J in Bryan, Texas.

CHAPTER 8

Greater Heights

★

Overall, 1943 brought more good news for the Allies than bad, and Americans grew optimistic about winning the war. But 1943 was a devastating year for B-17s and their crews. Ten percent of the planes that took off on bombing missions were lost, never to be seen again. Most of the ten crewmen aboard each of those planes were either killed or captured. Another 30 percent of the bombers were seriously damaged before returning to the Allies' bases. And in one horrific mission sixty B-17 Flying Fortresses were lost, along with the six hundred men in them.[118]

Plants in the United States built B-17s as fast as they could to meet the Army Air Forces' desperate need for the Flying Fortress bombers. Military commanders had to find more and more pilots, too. But men just coming out of flight training were a long way from being able to handle a Fortress.

In the meantime, the military still resisted having Wasps pilot bombers and other big planes, even as they continued to ferry smaller planes, tow targets and gliders, and teach men to fly. They couldn't be strong enough for the big planes, the generals said. Or big enough. Cochran kept pushing. And so did a few AAF instructors and commanders who had seen how skilled the Wasps were.

General William Tunner—who ran the Ferrying Division of the Army Air Forces and supported the idea of women pilots from the very beginning—thought Nancy Love and Betty Gillies would be the perfect pilots to demonstrate that women could, in fact, fly heavy bombers over long distances. If they succeeded, some of the men now ferrying the bombers in the United States could be moved to combat flights and the new B-17s could be put into action more quickly. Were Love and Gillies willing to train on the bomber? Absolutely.

The B-17 was a well-engineered plane known for flying smoothly and easily in a clear sky, but bad weather could make it clumsy in the air. And weighing thirty-five thousand pounds empty, and over sixty-five thousand with full fuel tanks and a load of bombs, it lumbered on the runway. Pilots had to fight the controls to keep the plane level in high winds. Strong men climbed out of the bomber's cockpit soaked with sweat and shaking with fatigue after those flights. Could even the most skilled women pilots handle the B-17?

For hours at a time Gillies and Love practiced controlling the powerful plane in the air, sometimes with one or two of its four engines intentionally shut down. They often landed with their arms and legs vibrating and their clothes dark with perspiration. But even the men who were certain no woman could fly a B-17 were impressed. Without wood blocks for the pedals and cushions under and behind her, five-feet-two-inch Betty Gillies couldn't operate the rudders or see over the control panel. She didn't weigh much more than a hundred pounds, yet she managed to keep the bomber straight and level using the engines on only one wing. The men had to admit that military command had been wrong about Wasps not being big enough or strong enough. Nancy Love and Betty Gillies had found ways to work around their size and strength and come out as good as the men flying missions in Europe or the Pacific.[119]

General Tunner kept Gillies's and Love's training on the B-17 a secret. They were the first women to train on a four-engine plane, and he didn't want the distraction of publicity. He had a plan for them once they were qualified on the bomber. Over a hundred B-17s were scheduled for transport to England as soon as they came off the assembly line. Though good pilots, the young men in the Ferrying Division who were scheduled to fly the bombers across the Atlantic were far less experienced than Love and Gillies. Many of them lacked confidence when it came to making a transatlantic flight in a plane they had just learned to fly. If Gillies and Love ferried a B-17 to England, Tunner thought, the young men would follow.

Tunner had good reason to think the women pilots could influence the men. Just weeks earlier one of Nancy Love's ferrying pilots had done just that at a base in New York. The men there were assigned to the P-39 Airacobra fighter, which they had taken to calling the "flying coffin" since several pilots were killed in P-39 crashes, usually on takeoff or landing. Some refused to fly the plane.

Then a woman assigned to the base asked for permission to take the fighter up. She studied the plane's manual carefully and practiced several takeoffs and landings, following the instructions' guidelines. She realized that the plane responded better when she landed it at a higher speed than she would with other types of planes. When she reported what she'd learned, it was discovered that many of the men piloting the fighter had not closely read the P-39 manual for takeoff and landing. Their failure to follow the instructions had caused many of the crashes. Once the pilots studied the manual and adjusted their takeoffs and landings, the accident rate for the plane dropped dramatically, saving both lives and needed aircraft.[120]

Tunner was sure that if a woman could convince the men to fly the P-39, Gillies and Love could do the same for the B-17.

Betty Gillies and Nancy Love were excited at the idea of taking a bomber to England. They knew they would enjoy the challenge and liked the idea of being the first women to fly such a plane. They may not have thought about it at the time, but that flight could help open doors for women in military aviation in a way that flying within the United States could not.

The flight was scheduled for early September. The route

would take the B-17 from Delaware to Maine, and then to Labrador, Canada, making the trip across the Atlantic as short as possible. Gillies and Love flew the plane as far as Labrador, with stops along the way, but as they and their male crew prepared to take off from Goose Bay, Labrador, they got a message canceling the flight. Hap Arnold, though he fully supported the WASP program in the United States, refused to allow the women to fly into a war zone.

Arnold may have feared the bad publicity if they were shot down. Or he may have worried that having women fly bombers across the ocean would hurt male pilots' morale. Whatever his reasoning, Gillies and Love were devastated. It seemed no amount of skill, no amount of training, and no amount of experience could get them past the barrier of being women—what's called the glass ceiling today. But their disappointment didn't slow them or their sister pilots down.

A month later at Lockbourne Army Air Base in Ohio, twenty-four-year-old Lieutenant Logue Mitchell learned that a group of Wasps was headed there for training on the B-17 so they could ferry the planes from factories to US bases. He would be the instructor for six of the seventeen women. Though Mitchell was young, he'd earned a reputation as an excellent flight instructor. He understood that different people learn in different ways, and he was fine with the idea of teaching Wasps to fly the four-engine Flying Fortress. Frances Green—who, before joining the WASP, had never been away from the small Texas town where she was born—said of the lieutenant, "He was firm, but he was compassionate. He was concerned. He did everything in the world he could to bring out the best in you."[121] The women couldn't have had a better teacher.

Mitchell had told his wife that it didn't take superhero strength to fly a B-17 bomber.[122] It took skill. He recognized that most women, even with exercise, did not have the muscle power of fit men, so he taught the Wasps how to put their hands palms up under the throttle instead of on top of it. The underhand hold reduced the strain on their shoulders. Slipping one foot under a rudder pedal when the leg on the other pedal starting shaking with fatigue released some pressure and gave leg muscles a few seconds to recover. However, tricks like that only went so far. The women needed to be as strong as they could be.

When they weren't in the air, Mitchell had them doing strengthening exercises. They tore folded newspapers and squeezed tennis balls to build muscles in their hands and wrists. And though lying on the floor under a cot and pushing it off the ground might have looked a little strange, it worked as well as any equipment in a gym to build shoulder and upper arm muscles.

Just as Betty and Nancy had flown the B-17 with one or two engines shut down as a regular part of their training, the new trainees did too. If both left engines or both right engines failed during an actual mission, a pilot had to be able to continue flying. Mitchell's students used what he'd taught them, but by the time they landed, they were ready to collapse from exhaustion anyway. The lieutenant assured them he'd seen plenty of big men do the same thing.[123]

Mitchell and the Wasps went up at night, and through storms, and in the cold. Over the roar of the engines they heard chunks of ice break off the propellers and slam into the sides of the uninsulated metal plane. They went above the clouds, higher than any of the women had flown before, and shivered in the twenty-degrees-below-zero air, and in altitudes so high there wasn't enough oxygen to breathe without a mask.

Unlike small one- or two-seat planes, the B-17 had a bathroom on board—sort of. A pilot or copilot could maneuver out of his or her harness, crawl through the two-foot opening behind the seats, step along the eight-inch catwalk above the bomb bay, walk past the radio desk, inch around the ball gunner's hatch, move between the machine gun platforms, and find in the far back of the plane a bottle and a funnel.

Frances Green realized on one night flight that she really needed to go. Her oxygen mask was connected to the big tank they all shared in the front, the tube only a few feet long. So Lieutenant Mitchell attached her breathing tube to a small bottle of oxygen and told her she had three minutes. No more. Frances found her way in the dark to the back of the plane and began working her way out of the layers of clothing she needed in the frigid altitude. Men who had to use the funnel could unzip those layers without removing them—a real time-saver. But it wasn't as easy for a woman. Frances worked as quickly as her cold fingers allowed. She nearly froze as she relieved herself and then stood up to start getting all those layers back on. The last garment was a pair of leather pants that zipped up the leg, but the zipper got stuck in her long johns. She tried to get it up. She tried to get it down. No luck.

The next thing Frances knew, she was waking up on the metal floor with someone holding an oxygen mask over her mouth and nose. "You were almost a goner," the young crewman staring at her said. Frances usually joked about everything. Not this time. If Lieutenant Mitchell hadn't set a stopwatch as she headed for the back of the plane, she would have died because of a faulty zipper and lack of oxygen.[124]

When the training course ended, thirteen of the seventeen women in Ohio checked out on the B-17. All of Lieutenant Mitchell's six women students passed their tests. More than that, they looked forward to piloting the bomber as much as possible. They felt confident and ready to take charge of the Flying Fortress. The men who had seen them pilot the plane in training knew they'd do well.

The military used dozens of different types of bombers during World War II, each designed for a particular purpose. The B-17 and several bombers developed later in the war were considered heavy bombers based on the size of the bomb load they could carry and the distance they could fly. All were four-engine planes.

Other bombers were classified as medium or light and were designed with two engines.

One widely used medium bomber was the B-26. Early in its service the accident rate for pilots training on the B-26 was high, and many pilots were hesitant to fly the plane. Wasps flew the B-26 at bases in Idaho and Alabama and did well. Most liked the aircraft despite its reputation. Like General Tunner in Delaware and the commander in Michigan, a commander in Alabama decided the Wasps could change the attitude of the men who refused to take the B-26 up.

Four Wasps who had trained on the B-26 were asked to fly two of the bombers over a base in Alabama and put on a bit of an air show for the hundreds of men in training who were on the ground. The trainees couldn't see who was flying the bombers in an impressive display of what the plane could do. When both planes landed smoothly and four women pilots climbed out of the cockpits, most of the men decided that maybe the B-26 wasn't so dangerous after all and they could learn to fly it.

Even after the success of the WASP demonstration, though, some women flying the B-26 ran into instructors and male pilots who welcomed them as pilots of military aircraft but still doubted women could fly bombers. A near disaster in Boise, Idaho, changed that opinion at one base.

Two Wasps who had been assigned to ferrying the B-26 went up as pilot and copilot in the bomber and had a good flight. But as they approached their landing, one of the two

Path to Victory in the Pacific, 1944

MANCHURIA

KOREA

JAPAN

N

P A C I F I C

CHINA

TAIWAN

O C E A N

PHILIPPINES

PHILIPPINE
SEA

MARIANA
ISLANDS

SAIPAN

GUAM

LEYTE
GULF

engines quit, leaving the plane unbalanced and extremely difficult to control. Sirens sounded as emergency equipment raced toward the runway, and everyone at the field turned to watch, afraid they were about to witness a tragedy. The women managed to turn the plane smoothly and started to bring it down toward the runway. However, the runway was narrow to begin with, and parked planes lined both sides of the pavement. If the bomber swerved or skidded at all, it could result in disaster.

The plane came lower and lower and finally touched down, straight as an arrow, taxiing to a stop as if both engines were humming. A fellow Wasp said later, "The cheer that went up after they landed! It was something to see and we were so proud of them!"[125]

As powerful as the B-26 and bigger B-17 bombers were, Hap Arnold and other AAF senior officers were convinced that the army needed a bigger class of bomber to defeat Japan without losing hundreds of thousands more American lives. Although the United States had bases in China, an ally in the war, the island nation of Japan was a very long flight for the planes of the 1940s. The weight of a loaded bomber required a tremendous amount of fuel, and a plane had to do more than get to its target—it had to get back home, too. Arnold was betting on a new aircraft as the way to meet the challenge—the B-29 Superfortress.

The B-29 was classified as a very heavy or long-range heavy bomber. It weighed twice as much as a B-17, and its wingspan was wider by almost forty feet—the length of a school bus. Most importantly, it could fly thirty-five hundred miles without refueling. By April 1944 there were enough B-29s and trained crews to launch an attack on Japan. If the navy and marines could capture the island of Saipan in the Pacific and build an airstrip there, the new bombers could fly over fifteen hundred miles to the Japanese homeland and make an Allied victory possible. News of the island's capture after a hard-fought battle came in July. By November an airstrip would be waiting for the B-29s and their crews.

The B-29 was a remarkable plane. Boeing had begun work on its design as the military began building its resources before the war. Even so, it took until late 1942 to build a prototype. The first of thousands of the new planes rolled off the assembly line in 1943 with little time for thorough testing. The pilots who flew the early B-29s found that the plane's engines tended to overheat and catch fire, often before takeoff. Naturally, once reports and rumors of those fires got out, pilots wanted nothing to do with the Superfortress, no matter how far it could fly.

Lieutenant Colonel Paul Tibbets—a twenty-five-year-old flight instructor for long-range heavy bombers—needed pilots for the B-29. But men who were afraid of the plane or uneasy about training on it didn't usually do very well. Tibbets had to have excellence. Having flown the plane himself, he believed skilled pilots could fly the B-29 safely. The trick was in understanding the plane. He just had to convince the men in his command he was right.

Tibbets decided to try the tactic that had gotten military pilots into the P-39, B-26, and B-17. He asked for two Wasp volunteers from a nearby base. Dora Dougherty and Didi Johnson said they'd be happy to fly the biggest four-engine bomber in production. Tibbets didn't discuss the fire hazard. Instead he told them to get the plane out of the hangar quickly after starting the engines and to take off right away—always. They did what they were told, and in just a few days of training with Tibbets, the Wasps were flying the B-29 smoothly. Lieutenant Colonel Tibbets decided they were ready for their check flight.

The women took off with Tibbets and an inspector from the Civil Aeronautics Administration on board. They did exactly as they'd been taught, but while they were demonstrating their ability to fly the plane with two engines shut down, the cockpit suddenly filled with smoke. One engine had caught fire!

Without hesitation Dora Dougherty gave clear instructions to everyone on board, radioed the tower for emergency equipment, and, with Didi as copilot, brought the plane down smoothly. When she climbed out of the cockpit onto the tarmac, the CAA inspector could hardly wait to sign her logbook, certifying her to fly the B-29. He'd never seen anyone do it better. [126]

Tibbets had had a B-29 set aside for the Wasps to use for demonstrations. The Fifinella mascot was painted in bright colors on the nose of the bomber, with the name Ladybird above it. Tibbets wanted to be sure the men watching the flights got the message: "So easy a girl can fly it." Dougherty and Johnson then went on a goodwill mission in their Ladybird. They flew generals, pilots, gunners, bombardiers, and all the other members of a bomber crew around New Mexico. "At stake was the ability of that aircraft to deliver the bomb it was built to fly," Dougherty said later. "It made me want to do a perfect job."[127] And she did.

As Dora Dougherty remembered,

> We completed our checkout by the end of the third
> day (despite an engine fire during the first flight)
> and thereafter demonstrated our ship, Ladybird,
> decorated with a painting of Fifinella on the nose, at
> the very heavy bomber training base at Alamogordo,
> New Mexico. After a short time, the purpose of the
> flights had been achieved. The male flight crews,
> their egos challenged, approached the B-29 with
> new enthusiasm and found it to be not a beast, but a
> smooth, delicately rigged, and responsive ship.[128]

Before long, though, the women were ordered to stop their tour. The head of the Air Staff in Washington, DC, was concerned that they were "putting the big football players to shame."[129] That was the end of Dora and Didi's flying career in the B-29. Only about a hundred pilots anywhere on Earth knew how to handle the Superfortress safely. Now the two who'd been assigned to convince other pilots to train on the plane were grounded as soon as the job was done. They were grounded because they were women and their ability as pilots might embarrass someone.[130]

The B-29 soon proved its worth. In March 1945 over three hundred B-29s took off from Saipan and flew about three thousand miles to Japan and back in the biggest air attack in history. The B-29 would bring the war closer to an end.

The Atomic Bomb

The United States was the first country to develop an atomic bomb. It was tested in New Mexico in July 1945, two months after Germany's surrender. Japan had continued to fight the war, and military leaders advised President Harry Truman (FDR had died in April 1945) that an invasion to defeat Japan would take another year of war and cost at least another one hundred thousand American lives. Truman decided to use the atomic bomb to force Japan's immediate surrender. Lieutenant Colonel Paul Tibbets was chosen to fly the B-29 bomber that would carry and drop the bomb on the city of Hiroshima. He called the plane the Enola Gay after his mother. On August 6, 1945, Tibbets and his crew dropped a single bomb more powerful than the combined force of all the bombs already dropped in the war. It destroyed 90 percent of Hiroshima and instantly killed over eighty thousand people. Tens of thousands more later died of radiation exposure. On August 9 the United States dropped a second bomb, on the city of Nagasaki. Six days later Japan surrendered. The nuclear age had begun.

• • •

At about the same time that women started flying the big bombers, Ann Baumgartner at Camp Davis learned she was being transferred. She certainly wasn't sorry to leave Davis. The harassment and dangerous discrimination there was nearly unbearable. Ann had done target towing, flown searchlight flights, and piloted drone mother ships. Now she and another Wasp got orders to report to Wright Field in Ohio to become experimental test pilots.

Wright Field was the biggest air force airplane testing center in the world. Engineers there experimented with every one of the million-plus parts of an aircraft to find the best materials and the best, most efficient designs. They experimented with pilots, too. How much force was safe when a plane took off? How high could a pilot fly before the lack of oxygen in the air had serious negative effects? How cold could a pilot be and still do the job? And did men and women react the same way to pressure, oxygen levels, and temperatures? That's where Ann Baumgartner and Betty Greene came in.

The two Wasps rode in a B-17 bomber above forty thousand feet with sensors taped to their bodies to measure temperature. They went into a pressure chamber and practiced writing their names in lower and lower oxygen levels to see the effect on their brains and coordination. They tried various kinds of equipment under different weather conditions. And finally, in the least glamorous assignment anywhere, they worked with a doctor to develop a way for women to urinate while strapped into a pilot's seat.

As Wasp Frances Green had learned when she almost died from lack of oxygen in a B-17 during training, the simple act of peeing had proved to be one of the most complicated problems Wasps faced. One woman said it was the worst thing she had to deal with as a pilot. The problem was especially serious in fighter planes, trainer planes, and other aircraft that had no toilets. Many had space for just one pilot and no other crew. Men used a tube they could slip into their unzipped flight suit without getting up. It collected their urine into a bag, which they disposed of later. A tube didn't work for women, no matter how many designs engineers tried.[131]

Unfortunately, Ann, Betty, and the female doctor they worked with couldn't develop a good solution either. Ann found that even the best design they came up with was inconvenient and difficult to use. Most Wasps chose to avoid taking in liquids before long flights. But aside from the discomfort that caused, dehydration

When a Pilot Has to Go

Until the twenty-first century, fighter pilots faced problems with urination during long flights. Various kinds of tubes, bags, and funnels failed to solve the problem because pilots had to wear multiple layers of thermal underwear, flight suits, G suits, and harness straps. Most female fighter pilots usually chose to wear adult diapers. In recent years engineers have developed male and female underwear fitted with a hose and pump that collects urine into a bag for disposal. Both men and women who fly fighter jets say the systems work well. The pilots are quite "relieved."

is dangerous and can make a person's thinking fuzzy, something a pilot can't afford. Needing fluids without having a good way to urinate made for a constant balancing act—one Ann wished she could solve.[132]

In every other way Ann's work at Wright Field was a great success. Betty Greene returned to Camp Davis when her assignment at Wright Field ended, but Ann Baumgartner accepted an offer to stay. She became the only woman to perform experimental military test flights at Wright, which made her the only woman pilot lucky enough to spend time with the elderly gentleman who frequently came to the test flight hangar to talk with the young flyers.[133] That elderly gentleman was none other than Orville Wright.

Still active and interested in new technologies and advances in flight, Orville Wright was particularly keen on the jet propulsion engines being tested at Wright Field, named for Orville and his brother Wilbur, who had died more than thirty years earlier. Engineers in Europe and the United States had been experimenting with jet, or turbine, engines for some time. They knew that a jet-powered plane would be able to fly faster than a plane powered by propellers. They believed jets would open a new chapter in flight. But any practical use of jet engines was so new, they hadn't been showcased at the New York World's Fair, which had closed less than four years earlier. The jet engine was now nearly ready for pilots to try, because World War II, like most wars, had pushed governments, scientists, and engineers to put all their efforts into developing war-related technologies as quickly as possible.

Jets—A New Kind of Thrust

The engines in a propeller plane create energy that turns the propellers. The propellers then produce thrust. In a jet the engines pull in air, compress it, and then use fuel to combust it (combustion occurs when certain kinds of fuel react with oxygen to release heat—this is why many fires can be extinguished by cutting off their oxygen supply, or smothering them). The exhaust produced by the combustion shoots out the back of the engine much faster than the colder air coming into the engines. This creates the thrust that pushes the plane forward. Think about running. As the runner sets her foot down, the muscles in her leg push, or thrust, her body forward.

Orville Wright wanted to see what this next generation of aircraft would be like. "Aviation will soar ahead," he told Ann, "though its progress between our 1903 flight and today still takes my breath away. Women even fly military planes now!"[134] Wright had no hesitation about women flying military planes. He asked Ann, "What kind of girl would want to fly an experimental jet? A pioneer like me, maybe?"[135]

Ann would never put herself in the same category as Orville Wright. He'd *invented* the airplane, for goodness' sake. He'd almost started aviation. But she wondered if she might be a kind of pioneer too. She got an answer in the fall of 1944 when she became a pioneer among pioneers as the only woman in a group of pilots scheduled to test-fly the Army Air Forces' first jet.

Ann wasn't near the head of the line waiting to fly the strange-looking craft on that bright October morning. That privilege was reserved for the colonels and majors who ran the testing program at Wright Field. Waiting was okay with her. No one knew exactly what to expect of a jet, including Ann. Watching someone else take off first seemed like a good idea.

It was the deafening noise of the jet engines everyone noticed right away. Their painfully high pitch was different from prop engines and sounded powerful in a way none of them had heard anywhere else. Ann and the others watched as the jet started taxiing on its first takeoff. It used more and more of the runway as it built speed. Would it ever leave the ground? And what about landing? They were told, "You'll have to land first time around. The slower acceleration of power in the jet will not get you off and around again."[136] No second chances. Ann hoped she was ready.

Finally it was her turn. She guided the jet down the runway in its long takeoff and felt the plane start to climb. But before it reached altitude, the roar of the engines stopped suddenly, as if they had stalled—as if they had shut down without warning. Ann felt a second of panic before realizing the plane was still climbing into the sky. Right. The noise of a jet engine is behind the pilot, where the turbines push the plane forward. She relaxed.

Ann's first experience of flying in near silence was astonishing. Something she would never forget. For thirty minutes or so she flew the only jet in American skies. And she knew she was the first woman to do it. However, she didn't know she would fly such a plane only once. Or that it would be nearly ten years before another woman flew a jet.[137] She didn't know her days as a WASP were coming to an end.

Baumgartner wasn't alone. Betty Gillies, Nancy Love, and the other Wasps flying huge bombers, pursuit planes, and trainer planes didn't know they'd be going home soon either. With factories continuing to send planes off assembly lines all over the country, men still being drafted into the military by the thousands, and a new group of women just beginning their classes at Avenger Field, every WASP and WASP trainee received two letters—one from Jacqueline Cochran and one from General Arnold. Both used gentle, kind words, but their message was harsh: The WASP program was over. By the end of the year, just two months away, there would be no more Wasps. Hap Arnold wrote, "I have directed that the WASP program be inactivated and all WASP be released on 20 December 1944."[138]

LIFE

368

AIR FORCE
PILOT

JULY 19, 1943 **10** CENTS
YEARLY SUBSCRIPTION $4.50

Shirley Slade, a **WASP** trainee, was featured on the cover of
Life magazine in 1943.

CHAPTER 9

Attacked

fter all they'd put up with and all their expectations of being militarized, the Wasps were being disbanded. Thrown out. Sent home. As if they'd done something wrong. "We were all done in to have it end so abruptly," one Wasp said. "We thought it would go until the end of the war."[139] The women were shocked. Most had had no idea their work was in jeopardy. So what had happened?

The simple answer is that the Wasps lost the battle for militarization. When Nancy Love and Jackie Cochran agreed to keep their programs civilian in 1942, they had expected militarization from Congress before too long. But a bill to militarize the women wasn't introduced in Congress until June 1944. It was defeated 188 to 169, and in August plans were made to end the program.

Simple answers, however, are not often complete. Congress had militarized all the other women's programs during the war. By 1944 there were nearly three hundred thousand women in the WAC, WAVES, and other groups with military status. They served in separate units from men, but they *were* military. And the bill to militarize the WASP had support from the Army Air Forces and the Department of War (today's Department of Defense). Congress had voted in favor of every single bill the AAF had asked for between 1941 and the WASP bill in 1944.[140] Why say no to the bill militarizing the Wasps? That answer is complicated.

For one thing, the Wasps' jobs were different from the jobs the other women's auxiliaries did. Most female members of the army, navy, coast guard, and marine auxiliaries did what was classified as "women's work." The work might be hard, even dangerous sometimes, and military men might have had those jobs before the war. But they were the kinds of jobs members of Congress and the public could imagine a woman doing: typists, bakers, secretaries, switchboard operators, nurses, and the like. All of those sounded like "women's work" even if they meant going into combat zones. Women in traditionally male jobs (doctors and engineers, for example) became part of the military too, though only in small numbers. And since women had taken over factory jobs and become mechanics in the civilian world, most people could swallow having women as mechanics for the military. Their country needed them.

The Wasps, on the other hand, weren't doing women's work. They were pilots. And most people thought of pilots, especially military pilots, as the manliest of manly men. Americans pictured their flyboys as dashing, handsome, and fearless. Sure, women could get pilot's licenses. They could be good small-plane pilots,

Rosie the Riveter: Image for an Era

The fictional Rosie the Riveter might be the most famous woman of World War II. But her past is complicated. The image most people have of Rosie comes from a poster showing a strong but feminine worker wearing a red polka-dot bandana. Her thought bubble says, "We Can Do It!" Yet this iconic war worker is not a riveter and has no name tag saying ROSIE. In fact, the poster was designed for the Westinghouse Electric Company to promote hard work. Using a woman on the poster was a big step, but the poster was never shown outside the Westinghouse plant. No one thought a thing about that image until it reappeared in the 1980s and became famous.

So where is World War II's real Rosie the Riveter? In 1943, American artist Norman Rockwell did a painting for a magazine cover that portrayed a strong, proud woman working as riveter. Her lunch box was labeled ROSIE, and Rosie the Riveter became a nickname for women in all kinds of war-related jobs. She even inspired a popular song. Today, Rosie the Riveter—usually seen in the Westinghouse poster version—is a symbol of feminism and women's determination and abilities.

and famous like Amelia Earhart and Jackie Cochran. But women flying military aircraft? That was something else and it put the Wasps in a more difficult position than other women's auxiliaries.

The timing of the request for militarization was another problem. In early 1942 the United States had been in real danger of defeat, and Americans supported every effort to win the war. A popular magazine editor echoed Franklin Roosevelt when he wrote, "There is terrible fighting to be done. All of us will be in the fight—men, women, and children."[141] Women, in particular, were encouraged to do their part and were admired for it. Most people saw women who went to work in factories and other war-related businesses as heroes (though they were paid less than men). Newspapers and magazines wrote articles on them. Posters and newsreels encouraged more women to join the workforce.

Those women, however, even those working in military auxiliaries early in the war, weren't *in* the military. Bills to give the Wacs, Waves, and SPARs (members of the Coast Guard Women's Reserve) military status in 1942 and 1943 passed, but they faced some opposition. A number of people still believed women just didn't belong in the military at all, no matter how womanlike their jobs were.

By the time the request to militarize the WASP was made in 1944, support for women's war efforts in both military and civilian work had shifted. The war was still raging on, but the Allies were closing in on Germany and Japan. An end was in sight, perhaps not even a year away, and Americans started asking what was going to happen when the war was over. Twelve million men in uniform would be coming home, which was wonderful news, of course. But what were those men going to do as civilians?

Where would so many young men find jobs all at once? People around the country assumed that those patriotic women who had stepped into men's jobs in 1941 and 1942 would step back out at the end of the war. They would go home to their families, or get married and start families. Whatever they did, they had to give all those jobs back to the men who had to support themselves and their wives and children. That belief left little enthusiasm for adding any more women to the military.

Additionally, with the Allies gaining the upper hand, strategies for winning the war changed and so did the military's need for soldiers. Early on, the only way to attack the enemy was from the air, and the AAF's terrible losses created an enormous need for pilots. By 1944, though, the war was being fought on the ground, so fewer planes and flight crews were needed, and fewer were being lost. The AAF began sending some pilots and crews home and were training fewer new men for those jobs.

With the ground war now the major focus in Europe, the army's need for ground forces *increased*. Bombing could prepare the way for the planned invasions, but in the end invasions meant fighting on land. There was nothing appealing about slogging through the mud wearing a seventy-pound backpack, or getting frostbite crawling through a mountain forest. But hundreds of thousands of foot soldiers were needed to do just that.

These changes led the Army Air Forces to close a number of flight schools, which meant that about nine hundred civilian instructors lost their jobs. They and a lot of other male civilian pilots had been excused from the draft while they used their civilian flying skills working for the military. Now, though, they could be called into the military to fill changing needs. General Arnold offered places in the AAF to any of the men who met the requirements. Many didn't, but a lot of those men did meet infantry standards, and they weren't happy about it since they didn't want to be foot soldiers.

Instructors, civilian pilots, and military men who were being turned down for military pilot's training quickly became the Wasps' biggest opponents. They wrote letters to Congress, spoke to veterans' organizations, and raised money to hire lobbyists who could influence members of Congress. Though most of the men were less experienced and less skilled as pilots than the Wasps, they wanted the Wasps' jobs. They thought they had a right to those jobs because they were men. Their efforts turned much of the public and many members of Congress against the WASP program.

The women pilots couldn't fight back to protect their jobs and their reputations. It wasn't that they didn't have strong arguments—they did—but they were under Jacqueline Cochran's orders to keep quiet, avoid interviews with the press, and not write to their representatives in Congress.[142]

This gag order had been issued in response to a series of articles in the press. While Jackie Cochran was quietly getting her program started in Texas in late 1942, magazine and newspaper editors and reporters heard about Nancy Love's pilots, who were already at work in Delaware. Journalists had done articles on women working in factories and on women's auxiliary military units like the WAC and WAVES. But few had known about the women working and training with the AAF. One writer learned of the women pilots when he was asked to give up his seat on a civilian flight so a ferrying pilot could get back to base. He was surprised when the pilot turned out to be a young woman.

"I saw that she was tired, desperately tired," the columnist wrote later in an article called "The Girls Deliver the Goods."

> She looked as if she hadn't slept in days. . . . I
> wondered how many flights she'd made in the past
> few days. . . . It was astonishing—humbling, too—
> to think of a girl like that flying Army planes to
> points all over the country, alone in the skies, hour
> after hour, flying through rain and sleet and snow
> and clouds.

That pilot so impressed him that he decided to visit New Castle, interview Nancy Love, and write about the program. His article appeared in a number of papers all over the country. It ended,

> I can hear a plane. . . . It's quite possible that
> somewhere up there, alone in the open cockpit of a
> trainer plane she is delivering, a girl is shivering in
> the wet wind, knowing she'll have to be alone and

cold for another seven or eight hours. She's flying up there, a mile above the earth, so that some man may be released to fight for his country.[143]

Photos appeared with the piece. They showed women pilots in their winter bomber jackets and leather helmets, and others in flight suits carrying their heavy gear. All complimentary and all business. That kind of article could be useful in gaining support for the programs in both Delaware and Texas, but unfortunately, businesslike articles were rare.

In July 1943, *Life* magazine did a cover story on the Wasps in Texas and their training at Avenger Field. The piece stuck to the business of the program for the most part. Titled "Girl Pilots," the article was accurate and complimentary in describing the women's long days and hard work, as well as their attitudes and abilities. "[They] fly with skill, precision and zest," it said, "their hearts set on piloting with an unfeminine purpose that might well be a threat to Hitler." The cover photo showed a WASP trainee in overalls, wearing no makeup and her hair in braids. Photos of the "girls" in their zoot suits, in classrooms and physical training, and at rest were included too. And the caption beneath a photo of Major General Martin Yount, head of the Army Air Forces Flying Training Command, quoted him as saying the Wasps were "qualified to replace all Army Air Force pilots in the noncombatant duties to which they will be assigned." All of that gave the public a serious and realistic picture of the Wasps.

Ladies Courageous

A Hollywood filmmaker produced a 1944 movie about the Women's Auxiliary Ferrying Squadron (the WAFS became part of the WASP in 1943). Though the film was made with the US Army Air Forces' permission, it was not a documentary, but a story with glamorous actresses and a bad script. A review in the *New York Times* said it portrayed the women pilots as "irresponsible nitwits" who steal planes, make intentional crash landings to get attention, and fight over one another's husbands. When a group of real WASPs went to see the movie in a town near their base, they were so humiliated by it that they sneaked out of the dark theater before it was over. The image portrayed in that film and in publications stuck with the public and hurt the WASPs in their effort to be militarized.

However, the *Life* article also used a photo of the women sunbathing behind the barracks. It was something the women did now and then, but readers weren't likely to see anything similar in articles about men flying for the military. The caption to a picture of Wasp Shirley Slade referred to her smiling "as her hair ruffles in Texas wind." And though Jacqueline Cochran was described as a famous pilot, she was also called "smart and pretty" and "glamorous."[144]

The same kind of language appeared in other publications. Reporters used adjectives like "attractive" or "comely" with nearly every mention of a Wasp. They remarked on the cut and style of their uniforms as if uniforms were mere fashion statements. The

Nurses in the News

Nurses during World War II often cared for the wounded under terrible and dangerous conditions. They saw horrible injuries and risked their own lives to save others. But the American public rarely saw what those women actually did. *Life* did articles on military nurses but did not include pictures of the women at work. Page after page of photographs showed the women at rest and at play. This kind of publicity gave readers a distorted view of military nurses and, like articles on the WASPs, emphasized the women's femininity rather than their real work.

fact was that uniforms provided identification and a kind of protection to Wasps on bases and around the country. The women were far less likely to be thrown out of a restaurant for wearing slacks if they were in uniforms rather than civilian clothes. And uniforms identified them as doing important work for the war effort when they arrived alone at hotels or train stations.

Instead of reporting on the women's skill, experience, and hard work, most articles focused on the women's figures and faces. They rarely described any actual flying and included staged photos of the most attractive women with their hair nicely styled and their flight suits clean and crisp. Those glamour-girl pieces gave the public a superficial and inaccurate view of the women's program.

The writers and editors of the glamour articles certainly knew they were presenting a shallow picture. The same thing had happened with articles about military nurses and even women on factory assembly lines. Somehow, no matter what work women did to aid the war effort, it was important to editors and readers that they remain traditionally feminine on the job.

But the writers and editors of articles like *Life*'s "Girl Pilots" may not have realized how often they focused on aspects of the women's lives that had nothing to do with their wartime work. That's how women were almost always treated in the press in the 1940s.

Life's editors may have intended their articles to be very supportive of women in the war effort, and in many ways they were. But the focus on girly information harmed the Wasps. "The girls are very serious about their chance to fly for the Army at Avenger Field," *Life* reported, "even when it means giving up nail polish, beauty parlors, and dates."[145]

Nail polish? Was that what the women were giving up to help fight the war? Or were they giving up the same things men serving the country in noncombat positions were giving up? Their spouses, their children, their homes, and their jobs. Was nail polish what Cornelia Fort gave up when she crashed into that Texas field?

The War Department in Washington, DC, reacted to the early glamour articles by banning most publicity on the WASP.[146] Jackie Cochran ordered the women to stay quiet and avoid interviews. But the limited articles published after that still managed to highlight hairstyles, dating, and figures—girly things—as though flying military aircraft with great skill wasn't as important as being pretty. Reporting on men usually focused on their work and heroism. Being handsome wasn't a requirement. These differences in articles on women and men left readers thinking of the Wasps as girls first and pilots second. No matter how much articles praised their skills and dedication, they were *girl* pilots, and that was distinctly different from the real thing.

The Wasps' gag order stayed in place while public opinion on women in the war effort shifted and the men who wanted the Wasps' jobs began their attack. The men had won over many publications and veterans' organizations. They argued to their representatives in Congress that the Wasps were taking jobs that should be theirs. One member of Congress who supported them, Representative Robert Ramspeck, decided to set up a committee to investigate.

No committee member—not one—ever visited Avenger

Have Times Changed?

Women in the United States Armed Forces in the twenty-first century have won Silver Stars, Bronze Stars, Purple Hearts, and many Combat Action Medals. They have been eligible to serve in all military jobs, including combat positions, since 2015. Their achievements have made the news. But as of 2017 very few books, films, or television shows about military conflicts have included women in major roles or as heroic military characters.[‡]

Lt. Gen. Nadja West, the highest-ranking woman to graduate from the US Military Academy.

Articles and reports on women in powerful positions in politics, business, and other areas continue to emphasize appearance. Hair and clothing are rarely a focus in articles or reports on men in similar roles. As a result, the public gains more information about male political candidates' positions on the issues than female candidates' positions. When women in politics speak forcefully, they are often called "shrill," a word not used about men. And women in politics or powerful business roles are frequently asked how they balance work and family life. Men rarely face that question.[§]

Field. No committee member ever went to a single base where Wasps were stationed. Two members talked to Nancy Love— once. They never talked to any other woman pilot. Yet the committee produced what seemed to be a detailed report. In reality, it was based on the male pilots' complaints, with no questions or skepticism from committee members.[147]

Some members of the committee disagreed with the report's conclusions and argued against them. They voted not to accept the Ramspeck Report. Nevertheless, a majority voted in support of it. The report concluded that the WASP program had never been necessary. It didn't mention that the War Department, the Army Air Forces, and General Arnold had all agreed and still agreed it *was* needed. The report argued that the women pilots' 80 percent graduation rate was low and proved that the money spent on the "costly and unnecessary program" was wasted. In fact, the Wasps' graduation rate was somewhat higher than that of the men in training, and the cost was about the same. The report also stated, "There is every reason to believe, that the induction of additional unskilled personnel will accelerate [increase] the accident and fatality rate." But Army Air Forces records showed the women had a lower accident and fatality rate than men, both in training and on missions.[148] The truth didn't seem to matter.

In the meantime, the House of Representatives' Committee on Appropriations, which decides how government money will be used for various programs, also issued a report on the Wasps. The members of the committee voted unanimously in favor of the report's conclusions. Those conclusions were the opposite of those in the negative Ramspeck Report and supported the AAF's request that the WASP be militarized.

> The members of the subcommittee . . . agree with General Arnold that [the Wasps] should be given military status and have the same responsibility as male pilots flying military airplanes, and, along with it, the same rights, privileges, and benefits to which such male pilots are entitled.[149]

The Appropriations Committee's report didn't make the news, but the Ramspeck Report did. Newspapers quoted it without checking its accuracy. The public had no way of knowing that the report they saw was filled with misinformation. Newspapers published opinion pieces attacking the WASP program as wasteful and worse. One referred to Jacqueline Cochran as "the shapely pilot" and suggested that General Arnold would do anything for her and the Wasps because of her "windblown bob [hair], smiling eyes and outdoor skin,"[150] as though the general had been swept away and had made terrible decisions because of Cochran's womanly charm. Another article said, "In colleges the smooth, good-looking gals can get A's without a lick of work; and in the armed services it may be that dimples have a devastating effect even on generals."[151] The reporter presented no evidence of attractive college women getting As without working for them, or any evidence that anyone in the military supported the Wasps because the women were pretty. Accusations like those were an enormous insult to both women and men.

Some newspapers did write in favor of keeping the WASP program. They described the excellent work the women were doing and their real records. Sadly, those papers were a minority.

The Wasps continued to fly as the debate went on. Many of them were unaware of what was happening in Congress. But the negative publicity in newspapers around the country had a devastating effect on the way a lot of men in the military or working as civilian pilots saw them. Wasps who had been welcomed and treated as equals at many bases suddenly found attitudes toward them changing. Long Beach, California, for example, had been one of the most welcoming bases in the country. Now, however, male flight instructors who wanted to be ferrying pilots but couldn't pass the tests yelled at the women and told them to go home. That kind of abuse was a shock. In North Carolina a Wasp was waiting for a bus when she was surrounded by several military men. They shouted at her and called her filthy names. When she moved toward the restroom, the men stood in her way. By the time her bus arrived, she was shaking and nauseous with fear.[152]

In mid-June, the whole House of Representatives began debate on the bill to militarize the Wasps. The entire Ramspeck Report, which had been finalized on June 5, was entered into evidence as fact. So were opinion columns from newspapers. Articles and editorials supporting the Wasps were ignored. The Wasps themselves couldn't speak up due to the gag order, but the men who opposed their militarization packed the Capitol's galleries and clapped and cheered as insults were thrown at the women.[153]

If the women had been asked to testify, they could have named the many commanders who asked for Wasps on their bases because their records were so good. They could have described the respect combat pilots had for them. Bob Morgan, an AAF captain who had piloted a B-17 bomber called the Memphis Belle had said, "We were short of pilots, and we needed all the combat pilots we could possibly have, and these gals could fly anything we could fly."[154] The women could have mentioned Lieutenant Colonel Paul Tibbets, who had trusted Wasps to demonstrate the B-29 to hesitant male pilots. The women could have told Congress about Orville Wright suggesting that Ann Baumgartner was a pioneer, but the Wasps weren't invited to the hearings, an invitation which would have overridden the gag order.

General Hap Arnold and the secretary of war testified in support of the Wasps. So did several members of Congress from the Military Affairs Committee who knew far more about the program than most other representatives, including those on the Ramspeck committee. They did their best, but accurate statistics and expert opinions didn't help convince representatives who listened only to what they wanted to hear. In the end the bill to militarize the Wasps was defeated. Was there anything else anyone could do? After a lot of thought Hap Arnold and Jackie Cochran decided there wasn't. In October they sent the devastating letters to all the Wasps.

On December 7, 1944, exactly three years after Cornelia

The Memphis Belle

The Memphis Belle gained fame as the first AAF heavy bomber of World War II to complete twenty-five missions with its crew alive and the plane still able to fly. In the early years of the war, such a record was real cause for celebration. The B-17 Flying Fortress bomber, named for the pilot's girlfriend in Memphis, Tennessee, returned to the United States in June 1943. Captain Robert Morgan and his crew continued to fly the Memphis Belle on a cross-country tour to sell war bonds and raise the public's morale. As of 2017 the Memphis Belle was being restored to be put on display at the National Museum of the United States Air Force near Dayton, Ohio.

Fort witnessed the attack on Pearl Harbor, General Hap Arnold addressed the last WASP graduating class at Avenger Field.

> You, and more than nine hundred of your sisters,
> have shown that you can fly wingtip to wingtip with
> your brothers. If ever there was a doubt in anyone's
> mind that women can become skillful pilots, the
> WASP have dispelled that doubt. . . .
>
> Frankly, I didn't know in 1941 whether a slip of
> a young girl could fight the controls of a B-17. . . .
>
> Well, now in 1944, more than two years since
> WASP first started flying with the Air Forces,
> we can come to only one conclusion—the entire
> operation has been a success. It is on the record
> that women can fly as well as men. . . .
>
> The Wasps have completed their mission. Their
> job has been successful. . . .
>
> . . . We of the AAF are proud of you; we will
> never forget our debt to you.

Those were heartfelt words, but they didn't change anything.

WASP trainees formed close bonds with each other and with Jacqueline Cochran, center.

CHAPTER 10

At Last

Teresa James was "heartbroken."[155] Betty Gillies was angry. Ann Baumgartner felt "incomplete" at not being able to continue to the war's end.[156] They'd been told success would lead to militarization. Instead the women who had proved they could fly anything men could fly were being sent home simply because they weren't men. "It was almost like a funeral," one Wasp said, "it was a shock. What do we do now?"[157]

"Their careers will be marriage," the WASP public relations officer told *Time*, a weekly news magazine. The women should go back to their husbands and live their lives on the ground like "ordinary" women. It was a tidy answer. But again things weren't that simple.

For many Wasps there was no going back. A lot of the women were single. Some married Wasps were now widowed, having lost husbands in the Pacific or in Europe. Teresa James's husband, who was called Dink, was a B-17 pilot shot down over France in June 1944 and listed as missing, presumed dead. James's and other

The Deadliest War in History

World War II was the deadliest, most destructive war in history. Nations around the world were involved. There is no way to determine the exact number of deaths the war caused worldwide, but estimates range from 60 to 80 million. Of those, the Soviet Union (today's Russia was the largest part of the Soviet Union) lost about 11 million soldiers and at least 7 million civilians out of a total population of 130 million. That's 14 percent. The United States, with about the same size population, suffered just over 400,000 military deaths and very few civilian deaths, since the war was not fought on American soil. The American loss was approximately 0.3 percent. In addition to war deaths, over 6 million Jews and other "inferior" people died in the Nazi Holocaust.

widowed pilots' careers in marriage had ended almost before they'd begun. As Wasps, they could share their sorrow, their fear, and their loneliness together. Now they were losing more than just their jobs; they were also losing one another. Teresa, one of the best of the best pilots anywhere, said later, "I'll never forget walking out the gate that morning."[158]

Most of the women got on with their lives, as they put it. Those with husbands and children were happy to be home, of course. They had missed their families terribly. Still, it wasn't easy to readjust to life on the ground, though one woman said, "History is history. It is good to remember our WASP experiences and to appreciate them, but what is present is more important and what is future is much more important."[159] Other Wasps felt the same way. They wished they'd been able to continue flying during the last year of the war. They had wanted to be part of the victory and the celebrations that followed. Some admitted they felt a little bitter about being denied those last months of service. Even so, when the men and women of the military, including the militarized women's auxiliaries, were honored as heroes in 1945, the Wasps joined with the rest of the country in cheering for them. Those men and women deserved to be called heroes. Former Wasps supported the laws giving those veterans benefits to help them go to college, buy houses, and get the health care they needed. But they resented not being honored or receiving benefits themselves. Hadn't they served their country by joining the WASP? And what about the thirty-eight Wasps who had died? Weren't they heroes too? It didn't seem right.

Some former Wasps, especially those who had started with Nancy Love in Delaware, blamed Jackie Cochran for the program's demise. They believed Cochran had waited too long to push for militarization. She'd also ordered the women to stay quiet when they should have been defending themselves. She'd been pushy, stubborn, selfish, and overconfident.

The majority of those who had trained in Texas, however, strongly defended Cochran. She'd lent many of them money to get to Avenger Field, and she'd designed and paid for their silver wings at graduation. Without her, they argued, the program wouldn't have existed beyond the handful of pilots in Nancy Love's ferrying squadron. Yes, Jacqueline Cochran was pushy and stubborn, but as Betty Jane Williams said, "If there was an obstacle Jackie knew how to get around it. That kind of gutsiness and aggressiveness in a woman is not always admired; in a man, it's applauded, not so in a woman."[160]

Whatever her faults, Cochran had given the Wasps an opportunity to soar, and many wanted to continue soaring. That public relations official might have told *Time* that marriage would be the women's career. And the majority of Wasps did marry. But did that mean marriage was really their *career*? The *Time* article acknowledged that military pilots weren't so sure the women would make marriage their career. As the men saw it, "Flying is a hard habit to break."[161] They were right.

Between 1942 and 1945 the war effort had forced industry to stop making appliances and the like, and switch to producing military equipment. It had encouraged women to take jobs outside the

The Women's Movement

In 1848 a small group of women in New York State organized a convention to demand the rights promised in the Declaration of Independence. They wanted the right to own and control property, to be educated, to hold jobs, to vote, and more. By the late 1800s their major goal was gaining suffrage—the right to vote. They achieved this in 1920 with the Nineteenth Amendment. But there was more to be done.

A second wave of the women's movement started in the 1960s. Women formed organizations to demand equal pay for equal work, an end to job discrimination, and access to universities, law schools, and medical schools. They campaigned for quality childcare and women's health care, including family planning. They made a great deal of progress.

In 1965 fewer than one in twenty-five girls played high school sports. Today that number is ten in twenty-five. Women in 1965 made up less than 10 percent of medical and law students. Nearly half of students in those fields today are women. But women continue to earn less than men on average, even in the same jobs. And complex issues remain. Many young women today consider themselves part of a third wave of the women's movement. They are confronting difficult questions concerning women in combat, abortion rights and issues, single mothers in poverty, sexual harassment, equal pay, and more.

home. But now with the war over, all that changed again. In the late 1940s industry was back to producing and marketing household goods, and women were expected to give up their wartime jobs for the millions of men coming back from the military. After all, the men needed those jobs and women really belonged in the home. Besides, all the new conveniences being advertised would make homemaking better than ever before.

Advertising, books and magazines, even radio and television shows, told women they should devote themselves to being full-time mothers and homemakers. Everywhere anyone looked were pictures and film of women happily cooking, cleaning, smiling at their children, and wanting nothing outside of that role. Companies like Westinghouse and General Electric had pushed the image of the glowing homemaker on women at the World's Fair before the war, and now they were pushing it again.

Dishwashers and clothes dryers were great, no doubt about it. So were frozen foods and all the rest. But while Betty Gillies, BJ Erickson, and many other former Wasps wouldn't have given up their families for anything, their hearts simply weren't in the kitchen or the laundry room. They were in the sky.

Teresa James tried to find work as an airline pilot after the Wasps were disbanded, but no civilian airline would hire her despite her stellar record. The same was true of most of the others who looked for jobs as pilots. Quite a few, including Ann Baumgartner and Gene Shaffer, found work as flight instructors, something many of them had done in the Civilian Pilot Training Program before the war. Some, like Lois Hollingsworth, opened flight schools. Betty Gillies went back to working as a pilot and test pilot for the aviation company where her husband worked, as she'd done before she joined the WASP. She also helped organize the All-Woman Transcontinental Air Race, known as the Powder Puff Derby. She and BJ Erickson and others competed in the race for years. Dora Dougherty, one of the best multiengine pilots Lieutenant Colonel Paul Tibbets had ever seen, became an instructor at the University of Illinois and set records as a helicopter pilot.

Most of the former Wasps, however, remained on the ground. Some stayed close to flight by working in the air industry. Betty Jane Williams moved to the new world of television, and wrote and filmed documentaries on aviation both for commercial television and as a nonflying officer in the Air Force Reserve. She won a dozen national awards for her documentaries.[162]

Others turned to new careers. One became a police officer, another a physicist.[163] There were authors and artists. But whatever they did, married or single, children or no children, the women stayed quiet about what they had done during World War II.

Shortly after the WASP program ended, the government closed the WASP records for a period of thirty years, making research almost impossible (the same was done with other war records once the war ended). Many of the women didn't even know exactly what had happened to force the end of the WASP. Those who did know the details weren't allowed to talk about them. The few women who tried to tell people what they had done during the war found people had never heard of the WASP and didn't believe their story. Gradually the public forgot the program had ever existed. Aside from an occasional conversation among old friends, no one talked about the WASP—not at all. Pilot Kaddy Steele, who had done target towing in Texas, said, "The WASP program was over; we got on with our lives, and nobody knew who we were and nobody cared."[164]

A small group of the women stayed active in the Order of the Fifinella, an organization founded as the Wasps were sent home. Finally, in 1964, one former Wasp decided to hold a reunion. The women who attended were glad to see one another again and talk about old times. It was like revisiting the most exciting part of their lives. They also realized how good it was to be able to talk about the shock and anger they'd felt at the way they'd been treated all those years ago. Some had never even told their children about their time in the air.

A few years later the women held a second reunion, and more Wasps attended. At the third reunion, in 1972, a larger group gathered. Over the years some Wasps had started working to get a bill before Congress that gave the group veterans' benefits. They'd had no success. As the women talked now, though, many of them agreed that it was time to do more. It had been thirty years since the program's start. They decided to demand what they'd been promised in 1942: militarization.[165]

This time the Wasps came together with know-how. They

were in their fifties and sixties, had raised families, and had succeeded in their careers and more. Additionally, they had some
powerful people on their side. Hap Arnold had died in 1950,
but his son—retired air force colonel Bruce Arnold—was happy

Women in the United States Air Force

The United States Air Force became a
separate branch of the armed forces in
1947. The following year the Women
in the Air Force (WAF) program was
established. Women could now serve
as a regular part of the air force but
were limited to ground duties. Several
former WASPs joined the USAF or
USAF Reserve, though they could not
be pilots despite their training and

experience flying military planes. In 1976 the USAF began accepting
women for pilot training. The United States Navy had trained its first
female pilots two years earlier, at the same time that the US Army began
training women as helicopter pilots.

to help. As a young lieutenant during the war, he'd seen the
Wasps fly target-towing patterns above the Mojave Desert at
Camp Irwin in California. They'd been willing to do what many
pilots assigned there refused to do—tow targets for gunner
trainees firing live ammunition from vehicles moving rapidly
over rough terrain. He had tremendous respect and admiration
for the Wasps and knew how much his father had respected and

admired these women too. They deserved recognition.

Senator Barry Goldwater of Arizona—who had been a military pilot during World War II—was on board as well. He'd worked with the women pilots and believed they'd earned veteran status. The women themselves began gathering documents, telling their stories, writing articles, and talking to members of Congress. It was still going to be an uphill battle. Some wondered if it was really worth fighting for militarization at this point at all.

In 1975, Congress passed legislation admitting women to the US military academies, including the Air Force Academy near Colorado Springs, Colorado. The next year the air force proudly announced that the USAF would begin training American women to fly military aircraft for the first time. Women training to fly military aircraft for the *first* time? Were they joking? Hap Arnold had said in 1944 that the service the WASP had given would never be forgotten. Apparently, he'd been wrong.

Former Wasp Kaddy Steele described the women's reaction. "When . . . they made the announcement . . . it really set a bomb under all of us."[166]

"We stepped up and pushed the envelope, and then had to back up a little and wait for total acceptance. Society wasn't ready," one Wasp explained.[167] But society had changed by the late 1970s, and the women were determined to achieve "total acceptance" now.

The Wasps had fought for themselves as women pilots in a

man's world during the war. They could do it again. They'd fight for themselves and for their sister pilots killed in action. They'd fight for those who had died since 1944. And for the women who needed the financial and medical benefits veterans received. They'd fight for every one of the 1,102 forgotten Wasps. And for the truth.

Opposition from some veterans' organizations and members of Congress hadn't weakened over time. But the women formed a WASP Military Committee, chaired by Colonel Bruce Arnold, and got to work. Americans' views of women were changing, and Wasps were able to collect signatures on petitions all over the country. Dora Dougherty created fact sheets and handed them out to hundreds of people standing in line to see a new movie called *Star Wars*. Moviegoers were polite to the soft-spoken, middle-aged woman. Then, astonished at the information she gave them, they eagerly signed her petition to Congress. Dougherty went back again and again and collected thousands of signatures.[168] Many Wasps wrote to their representatives and to newspapers, the very thing they had not been allowed to do in 1944. Marie Muccie, who had laughed at herself in her gigantic military zoot suit, argued,

> Opponents of the bill say we Wasps were not under
> military discipline. They must be kidding. We
> received the same training as the male Air Force
> Cadets. The US Army Air Corps issued orders for

all military missions. We flew all the same type military aircraft from small trainers to bombers. . . .

. . . By offering official recognition of our part to help win the war would mean a great deal to us. It would be like the US government saying, "Thank you for a job well done." We earned it, we deserve it and we did do a good job.[169]

Dora Dougherty traveled to Washington and testified before Congress in September 1977. Now a lieutenant colonel in the Air Force Reserve, a record-setting test pilot, and department chief at Bell Helicopter, she told the Senate committee, "We have waited many years to tell our story."[170] As of 1975 the WASP records that had been closed in 1944 were opened, and Dougherty and other former Wasps gained access to documents showing they had been treated like military personnel. They described their experiences flying with male officers and having base commanders assume they, too, were military. They reminded the committee of the women who had died in action.

Former commanding officers did the same, one bringing over a hundred pages of evidence that the women had been treated the same way military personnel were.[171] Colonel Arnold spoke passionately about the women's service. He pointed out that they had taken greater risks than many military personnel who worked in offices and supply depots and other positions and who now had veteran status and veterans' benefits.

Who is more deserving, a young girl, flying on
written official military orders, who is shot down
and killed by our own anti-aircraft artillery while
carrying out those orders, or a young finance clerk
with an eight to five job in a Denver office?[172]

Still, committee members hesitated. Was there documenta-
tion, written proof, that the AAF had considered the WASP de
facto military—not just *like* the military, but an actual part of the
military, even though they hadn't been militarized by Congress?

In 1944 pilot Helen Porter had been the only Wasp assigned to
Strother Field in Kansas.[173] When she got the letters from General Arnold and Jacqueline Cochran and learned that the program would soon end, she decided to resign rather than wait until
December. Arnold had ordered AAF commanding officers to
give the Wasps some sort of discharge papers when they left the
program. It was up to the commanders to decide exactly what the
papers said. Helen's commander used a regular army discharge
form and filled it in, saying, "This is to certify that Helen Porter
honorably served in active Federal Service in the Army of the
United States."[174]

By 1977, Helen lived on a farm in Pennsylvania where she
raised Appaloosa horses. She also worked as a flight instructor
and flew search-and-rescue missions.[175] Now she had the chance
to rescue her fellow Wasps. Helen had kept her discharge paper

and happily turned it over to the women of the WASP Military Committee.

Would the air force say the Wasps were de facto military? Yes. Porter's discharge paper was a major support for that position. And members of Congress couldn't deny that it was identical to the discharge papers so many of them had at home.

The Armed Forces' Precision Flying Teams

The US Navy Blue Angels and the US Air Force Thunderbirds are flight squadrons who demonstrate the military's aircraft and their pilots' skills at air shows around the country. The teams' mission is to make a connection between the military and the American public, and to boost interest and pride in the military. Many military pilots say they decided to become pilots after seeing the Blue Angels or the Thunderbirds—much like the pilots of the 1930s and 1940s who were inspired by the daring skill of barnstormers.

. . .

In November 1977, thirty-five years after the WASP program had started, Congress passed and President Jimmy Carter signed a bill authorizing the Women Airforce Service Pilots to "have their service recognized as active military service . . . and to receive honorable discharges and full veterans' benefits."[176]

The Wasps felt like they were finally soaring again.

Elaine Harmon, age eighty-six, in a T-6 cockpit in August 2006.

Epilogue

I n March 2010 nearly two hundred former Wasps gathered at the Capitol in Washington, DC. They weren't there to protest or make demands this time. Now in their late eighties and nineties, they came for themselves and to represent the one hundred surviving Wasps who could not make the trip. They came to represent the nearly eight hundred who were no longer living. On behalf of all 1,102 Women Airforce Service Pilots, these women were at the Capitol to receive the Congressional Gold Medal—the highest honor Congress can award to civilians.

Women had made great strides in military service and military aviation since the Wasps were sent home in 1944. They became a permanent part of the military with the passage of the Women's Armed Services Integration Act in 1948, meaning there would be no more special bills to militarize women job by job. In 1976 the military academies opened to women, and shortly after, women began training as air force pilots. The navy and army accepted women pilots as well. Ten years later women were flying refueling missions to support combat flights in North Africa. In the early 1990s, Congress ended laws banning women pilots from combat missions. At about the same time, the first woman member of the military to go into space—Major Susan Helms—flew aboard the space shuttle *Endeavor*.

Since the days of Amelia Earhart and Jackie Cochran, each achievement by a woman aviator had inspired other women to reach new heights. The Wasps were a strong part of that chain. If they ever doubted their influence, they had only to look at Major Nicole Malachowski. In 2006 she became the first woman pilot to fly as part of the USAF's precision flying team, the Thunderbirds. Her handle, the nickname she chose, was Fifi—in honor of the WASP and the mascot Fifinella. As she said, "The airplane is the greatest equalizer in the world."[177]

Malachowski was at the Capitol in 2010 to address the Gold Medal recipients and their audience.

> Their motive for wanting to fly airplanes all those
> years ago wasn't for fame or glory or recognition.
> They simply had a passion to take what gifts they
> had and use them to help defend not only America,
> but the entire free world, from tyranny. . . . And
> they let no one get in their way.[178]

The former Wasps in attendance, some now using canes or walkers or wheelchairs, agreed. "It's almost unbelievable," Betty

Wall Strohfus said. "We never thought this day would come. We were all just so grateful to have the opportunity to fly."[179]

Others had expressed the same feelings. According to Kaddy Steele, "[Flying for the AAF] was the high point of our life—bigger than going to college, bigger than getting your first job, bigger than getting married."[180] Another claimed, "I can honestly say that the Wasps prepared me for the rest of my life. Challenges will always be challenges, and I learned that hard work is what helps a person meet those challenges."[181]

Wasp Elaine Harmon knew all about the value of hard work. She'd worked hard to get her pilot's license and fly as a Wasp, and worked hard again with the WASP Military Committee to gain recognition and benefits for her sister pilots. In late 2009, her thick white hair framing her wide smile, she stood proudly behind President Barack Obama in the Oval Office as he signed the bill awarding the women the Congressional Gold Medal. She then stood proudly at the March ceremony. But she wasn't finished yet.

The 1977 bill had given Wasps military status and the benefits administered by the Department of Veterans Affairs. Finally their families could honor them with a flag-draped casket without breaking any rules. They could be buried with military honors, and many chose to be interred at army national cemeteries around the country.

Arlington National Cemetery, the most prestigious and well-known burial site for military veterans in the nation, overlooks Washington, DC, from the Virginia side of the Potomac River.

Unlike other national military cemeteries, it is administered by the United States Army rather than the Department of Veterans Affairs. After some argument about whether the 1977 law applied to Arlington, several Wasps were buried there, including Dora Dougherty, who had demonstrated the B-29. Still the debate wasn't over. When Elaine Harmon died in 2015 at the age of ninety-five, her children found a handwritten note in their mother's fireproof documents box. Written on notepaper imprinted with the WASP silver wings at the top and the Fifinella mascot in one corner, it said, "I would like to be buried in Arlington Cemetery," and went on to explain where the family would find the required discharge papers.

Just a month earlier a new secretary of the army had determined that the 1977 law militarizing the WASP applied only to benefits and privileges overseen by the Department of Veterans Affairs. He argued that the army did not have legal authority to grant Harmon's request and she could not be buried at Arlington. But Harmon, who had raised her four children alone after her husband died when they were young, had taught them to be as determined as she was. She had never taken no for an answer, and her children and grandchildren weren't going to either.

The Harmon family organized to fight for the woman they held dear. They started a petition and eventually got over 178,000 signatures. They enlisted two members of Congress to fight on their behalf—both veterans and both women. Representative Martha McSally, the first woman air force fighter pilot to fly in combat, said, "These women were getting a last slap in the face. I said, 'No way.'"[182] She and Iraq War veteran Joni Ernst sponsored a bill in the House of Representatives, and Maryland Senator Barbara Mikulski did the same in the Senate.

In 2016, Elaine Harmon and all the Wasps earned one more proud, smiling moment as President Obama signed into law a bill clearing the way for the women to be interred with full military honors at Arlington National Cemetery. Wasps who were able to travel came from near and far to witness Harmon's burial. As one said, "I wanted to be here to make sure they didn't fuss it up."[183] Finally Wasp Elaine Harmon was laid to rest, her work done.

The journey had been a long one. The Wasps had flown sixty million miles in seventy-eight different types of aircraft and then waited seventy-four years for full recognition. Was it worth all the effort to serve as pilots during the war in the first place? Was it worth all the effort to gain recognition after the war? Would the Wasps choose to be part of the Women Airforce Service Pilots again if they had the chance?

Most agreed at the time, and still agreed seventy years later, that despite the challenges, hard work, danger, discomfort, and discrimination they faced, their time in the air had been the best time of their lives. They loved it. Moreover, flying for the United States of America against the forces of tyranny was an honor and a privilege.

As Gene Shaffer FitzPatrick put it, "You bet your sweet life, I'd do it again."[184]

Bibliography

American Studies at the University of Virginia. "Welcome to Tomorrow." Accessed July 18, 2016. http://xroads.virginia.edu/~1930s/display/39wf /frame.htm.

Andy's WASP Web Pages. "Marie Muccie Genaro, WASP, Class 43-2." Last modified January 25, 2003. http://www.wwii-women-pilots.org/marie -genaro-43-2.html.

"Army & Navy: Home by Christmas," *Time*, 16 October, 1944. content.time .com/time/magazine/0,9263,7601441016,00.html.

Arnold, Hap. "Notification of the End of the WASP Program." October 1, 1944. Accessed January 11, 2016. PBS online. http://www.pbs.org/wgbh /amex/flygirls/filmmore/reference/primary/officialcorr05.html.

Atlanta Journal-Constitution online. "World War II: A Timeline of American Casualties." September 2015. http://www.ajc.com/news/anniversary -world-war-2/.

BBC Archive. "The Transcript of Neville Chamberlain's Declaration of War." Broadcast September 3, 1939. http://www.bbc.co.uk/archive/ww2outbreak /7957.shtml?page=txt.

Buzanowski, J. G. "First Female Military Pilots Get Congressional Gold Medal." *DoD News*. US Department of Defense. March 11, 2010. http:// archive.defense.gov/news/newsarticle.aspx?id=58279.

Carl, Ann B. *A WASP Among Eagles: A Woman Military Test Pilot in World War II*. Washington, DC: Smithsonian Institution Press, 1999.

Churchill, Winston. "We Shall Fight on the Beaches." Report to the House of Commons, June 4, 1940. The International Churchill Society. http://www .winstonchurchill.org/resources/speeches/1940-the-finest-hour/128-we -shall-fight-on-the-beaches.

Cochran, Jacqueline. *Report on Women's Pilot Program*. Wings Across America. Accessed April 27, 2017. http://wingsacrossamerica.us/records_all /DOCUMENTS/final_report.htm

Collins, Bob. "How a Saint Paul–Born 'Fly Girl' Changed History." *NewsCut* (blog). November 25, 2013. http://blogs.mprnews.org/newscut/2013/11/how -a-saint-paul-born-flygirl-changed-history/.

Comm. on Appropriations. Military Establishment Appropriation Bill for 1945. H. R. Rep. No. 1606-78 (1944).

Comulada, Jon. "Meet Elaine Harmon, a WWII Veteran with a Unique Dying Wish." Upworthy. September 8, 2016. http://www.upworthy.com/meet -elaine-harmon-a-wwii-veteran-with-a-unique-dying-wish.

Deseret News. "Death: Frances Green Kari." May 19, 1994. http://www .deseretnews.com/article/354003/DEATH--FRANCES-GREEN-KARI .html?pg=all.

Dumovich, Eve. "True Trailblazers." Historical Perspective. *Boeing Frontiers* 6, no. 10 (March 2008): 8–9. http://www.boeing.com/news/frontiers /archive/2008/march/i_history.pdf.

Fandos, Nicholas. "A Female World War II Pilot Is Finally an Equal at Arlington." *New York Times.* September 7, 2016. http://www.nytimes.com /2016/09/08/us/arlington-female-pilot-elaine-harmon-buried-at-arlington .html?_r=0.

Garber, Megan. "Night Witches: The Female Fighter Pilots of World War II." *The Atlantic.* July 15, 2013. Accessed July 30, 2017. https://www.theatlantic .com/technology/archive/2013/07/night-witches-the-female-fighter-pilots-of -world-war-ii/277779/.

Goodwin, Doris Kearns. *No Ordinary Time: Franklin and Eleanor Roosevelt; The Home Front in World War II.* New York: Simon and Schuster, 1994.

Grosscup, Luann. "Fly Girls: Wasps Carried the Non-combat Load When the Boys Were 'Over There.'" *Chicago Tribune.* May 23, 1999. http:// articles.chicagotribune.com/1999-05-23/travel/9907100180_1_women -airforce-service-pilots-wasps-military-pilots.

History.com. "American Women in World War II." 2010. http://www.history .com/topics/world-war-ii/american-women-in-world-war-ii.

Holbrook, Stett. "Coastside Woman Part of Secret Flying Force." *Half Moon Bay Review.* October 3, 1997. http://www.hmbreview.com/coastside-woman -part-of-secret-flying-forcestett-holbrook-half-moon/article_53d798f6 -90ec-5025-ab22-502c1f2a1626.html.

Jean, Pamela. "Fallen Hero: Fly Girl from Kalamazoo." *Everyday Citizen.* May 28, 2007. http://www.everydaycitizen.com/2007/05/my_aunt_mabel _my_hero.html.

Kari, Francis G. Interview. Story Commons. May 24, 1993. https:// lifestorycommons.wordpress.com/stories/frances-green-krri/.

Keil, Sally Van Wagenen. *Those Wonderful Women in Their Flying Machines: The Unknown Heroines of World War II.* New York: Four Directions Press, 1990.

Ladevich, Laurel. "Fly Girls." *American Experience*, season 11, episode 9. Directed by Laurel Ladevich. Aired May 10, 1999. Arlington, VA: PBS Home Video, 1999. DVD.

Lemmon, Gayle Tzemach. "Missing in Action." *Atlantic*. August 4, 2015. https://www.theatlantic.com/entertainment/archive/2015/08/missing-in -action/400235/.

Life. "Girl Pilots." July 19, 1943. https://books.google.com/books?id= MVAEAAAAMBAJ&printsec=frontcover&source=gbs_ge_summary _r&cad=0#v=onepage&q&f=false.

Merryman, Molly. *Clipped Wings: The Rise and Fall of the Women Airforce Service Pilots (Wasps) of World War II*. New York: New York University Press, 1998.

"Militarization of the Wasps," *Fly Girls*, American Experience [online]. http:// www.pbs.org/wgbh/amex/flygirls/peopleevents/pandeAMEX08.html

Mondey, David. *The Hamlin Concise Guide to American Aircraft of World War II*. Edison, NJ: Chartwell Books, 1982.

Nathan, Amy. *Yankee Doodle Gals: Women Pilots of World War II*. Washington, DC: National Geographic Society, 2001.

National World War II Museum. "By the Numbers: The U.S. Military." Accessed April 12, 2017. http://www.nationalww2museum.org/learn /education/for-students/ww2-history/ww2-by-the-numbers/us-military .html.

New York Times. "President Opens Fair as a Symbol of Peace." April 30, 1939. http://www.nytimes.com/times-insider/2014/04/30/april-30-1939-the -new-york-worlds-fair-opens-to-the-public/.

Official Archive Women Airforce Service Pilots. "WASP Assigned Duty Bases and Their Location." Texas Women's University Libraries. Last modified April 21, 2017. http://www.twu.edu/downloads/library/WASP_AT_WASP _Assigned_Bases.pdf.

Pantti, Mervi. "Literary Review for the Project Gender, Politics and Media: Challenging Stereotypes, Promoting Diversity, Strengthening Equality." Last modified April 7, 2006. Portraying Politics. http://www.portrayingpolitics .org/research2.php#24.

Paul Tibbets, interview by Dawn Letson, Women Airforce Service Pilots Oral History Project. February 4, 1997.

PBS online. "War Production." September 2007. http://www.pbs.org/thewar /at_home_war_production.htm.

Pisano, Dominick, ed. *The Airplane in American Culture*. Ann Arbor: University of Michigan Press, 2003.

Pohly, Pam. "Mabel Virginia Rawlinson." Mary Creason's Aviation. April 20, 2017. http://wingsacrossamerica.us/web/obits/rawlinsom_mabel.htm.

Ricci, Lola Perkins, ed. *WASP Newsletter* 10 (December 1974). http://www.twu.edu/library/wasp/newsletters/1974_Dec.pdf.

Roosevelt, Eleanor. "My Day: September 1, 1942." The Eleanor Roosevelt Papers Digital Edition. 2008. https://www.gwu.edu/~erpapers/myday/displaydoc.cfm?_y=1942&_f=md056279.

Rowland, Ashley. "Pioneer Female Pilot to Share Story." *Gainesville Sun*. December 14, 2002. http://www.gainesville.com/news/20021214/pioneer-female-pilot-to-share-story.

Rowley, Betty. "Teresa James: Pioneer Pilot." Ninety-Nines. June 1, 2009. http://www.ninety-nines.org/teresa-james.htm.

Schisgall, Oscar. "The Girls Deliver the Goods." *Cincinnati Enquirer*. February 28, 1943. https://www.newspapers.com/image/100467314.

Schrader, Helena Page. *Sisters in Arms: British and American Women Pilots During World War II*. Barnsley, UK: Pen and Sword Aviation, 2006.

Simbeck, Rob. *Daughter of the Air: The Brief, Soaring Life of Cornelia Fort*. New York: Atlantic Monthly Press, 1999.

Strebe, Amy Goodpaster. *Flying for Her Country: The American and Soviet Women Military Pilots of World War II*. Westport, CT: Praeger Security International, 2007. https://books.google.com/books?id=bFbUVQNeSwoC&pg=PA6&lpg=PA6&dq=cochran+lunch+with+arnold+1941&source=bl&ots=1DknKIHm0d&sig=RfAi8CTXvUrHgITl_llsapBiISA&hl=en&sa=X&ved=0ahUKEwijhNbnktXLAhUM7yYKHWsdD_8Q6AEIOzAG#v=onepage&q=cochran%20lunch%20with%20arnold%201941&f=false.

Strother, Dora Dougherty. "Women of the WASP." Introduction to *For God, Country, and the Thrill of It*, by Anne Noggle. College Station: Texas A&M University Press, 1990. http://www.wingsacrossamerica.us/records_all/wasp_articles/strother.pdf.

Tekeei, Negar. "Fly Girl." *Northwestern*. Spring 2002. http://www.northwestern.edu/magazine/northwestern/spring2002/features/flygirl/.

Tindall, George Brown, and David E. Shi. *America: A Narrative History*. New York: W. W. Norton, 1997.

US Department of Defense. "Description of Medals." Accessed January 23, 2017. http://valor.defense.gov/Description-of-Awards/.

Verges, Marianne. *On Silver Wings: The Woman Airforce Service Pilots of World War II, 1942–1944*. New York: Ballantine Books, 1991.

WASP Final Flight (blog). "WASP Betty Jane Williams, 44-W-6." December 8, 2008. http://waspfinalflight.blogspot.com/2008/12/wasp-betty-jane-williams-44-w-6.html.

Williams, Vera S. *Wasps: Women Airforce Service Pilots of World War II*. Osceola, WI: Motorbooks International, 1994.

Wolff, Scott. "Warrior Wednesday: Lieutenant Colonel Nicole 'Fifi' Malachowski." FighterSweep.com. March 18, 2015. https://fightersweep.com/1670/warrior-wednesday-lieutenant-colonel-nicole-fifi-malachowski/.

Woolner, David. "The 'Special Relationship' Between Great Britain and the United States Began with FDR." Roosevelt Forward. July 22, 2010. http://rooseveltinstitute.org/special-relationship-between-great-britain-and-united-states-began-fdr/.

World War II Foundation. "World War II Aircraft Facts." 2016. http://www.wwiifoundation.org/students/wwii-aircraft-facts/.

Yellin, Emily. *Our Mothers' War: American Women at Home and at the Front During World War II*. New York: Free Press, 2004.

Zimmerman, Dwight Jon. "Automobile Factories Switched to War Production as America Entered World War II." Defense Media Network. February 10, 2012. http://www.defensemedianetwork.com/stories/automobile-factories-switched-to-war-production-as-america-entered-world-war-ii/.

Notes

Main Text

1. *New York Times*, "President Opens Fair."
2. American Studies at the University of Virginia, "Welcome to Tomorrow."
3. Carl, *A WASP Among Eagles*, 20–21.
4. Ibid., 21.
5. BBC Archive, "Chamberlain's Declaration of War."
6. Carl, *A WASP Among Eagles*, 21–22.
7. Ibid., 21.
8. Nathan, *Yankee Doodle Gals*, 17.
9. Cochran, Report on Women's Pilot Program, 57.
10. Ladevich, "Fly Girls."
11. Keil, *Those Wonderful Women*, 47.
12. National Museum of the United States Air Force, "Women Airforce Service Pilots."
13. Keil, *Those Wonderful Women*, 51.
14. Ibid., 108.
15. Ibid., 330.
16. Merryman, *Clipped Wings*, 11.
17. Carl, *A WASP Among Eagles*, 21.
18. Churchill, "We Shall Fight."
19. Woolner, "'Special Relationship.'"
20. Keil, *Those Wonderful Women*, 52.
21. Cochran, *The Autobiography of the greatest Woman Pilot in Aviation History*, 169.
22. Ibid., 170–71.
23. Keil, *Those Wonderful Women*, 52–53.
24. Simbeck, *Daughter of the Air*, 111.
25. Ibid., 30, 37.
26. Ibid., 76–77, 87.
27. Ibid., 2.
28. Ibid., 3–4.
29. Goodwin, *No Ordinary Time*, 231.
30. Ibid., 316.
31. Zimmerman, "Automobile Factories."

32. PBS online, "War Production."

33. Goodwin, *No Ordinary Time*, 291.

34. History.com, "American Women in World War II."

35. National World War II Museum, "By the Numbers."

36. Simbeck, *Daughter of the Air*, 107.

37. Keil, *Those Wonderful Women*, 109.

38. Simbeck, *Daughter of the Air*, 108.

39. Ibid., 115.

40. Tindall and Shi, *America: A Narrative History*, 907.

41. *Atlanta Journal-Constitution* online, "World War II: A Timeline."

42. Keil, *Those Wonderful Women*, 118.

43. Roosevelt, "My Day."

44. Simbeck, *Daughter of the Air*, 121.

45. Ibid., 138.

46. Williams, *Wasps*, 71.

47. Simbeck, *Daughter of the Air*, 137.

48. Ibid., 135.

49. Ibid., 134.

50. Keil, *Those Wonderful Women*, 127.

51. Ibid., 128.

52. Simbeck, *Daughter of the Air*, 152.

53. Ibid., 153.

54. Keil, *Those Wonderful Women*, 145.

55. Verges, *On Silver Wings*, 72.

56. Merryman, *Clipped Wings*, 16.

57. Keil, *Those Wonderful Women*, 166.

58. Ibid., 146.

59. Williams, *Wasps*, 115.

60. Verges, *On Silver Wings*, 75–76.

61. Ibid., 77.

62. Ibid., 79.

63. Keil, *Those Wonderful Women*, 148.

64. Ibid.

65. Williams, *Wasps*, 51.

66. Carl, *A WASP Among Eagles*, 23.

67. Ibid., 23–25.

68. Keil, *Those Wonderful* Women, 154–155.

69. Ladevich, "Fly Girls."

70. Williams, *Wasps*, 71.

71. Ibid.

72. Keil, *Those Wonderful Women*, 161.

73. Cochran, 353.

74. Carl, *A WASP Among Eagles*, 50.

75. Merryman, *Clipped Wings*, 107.

76. Schrader, *Sisters in Arms*, 179.

77. Keil, *Those Wonderful Women*, 165.

78. Williams, *Wasps*, 28.

79. Merryman, *Clipped Wings*, 15.

80. Ladevich, "Fly Girls."

81. Williams, *Wasps*, 91.

82. Keil, *Those Wonderful Women*, 261–62.

83. Ibid., 257–258.

84. Ibid., 134–35.

85. Ibid., 136–137.

86. Williams, *Wasps*, 93.

87. Simbeck, *Daughter of the Air*, 227–28.

88. Ibid., 234–35.

89. Schrader, *Sisters in Arms*, 108.

90. Simbeck, *Daughter of the Air*, 153.

91. Carl, *A WASP Among Eagles*, 52.

92. Merryman, *Clipped Wings*, 25.

93. Rowland, "Pioneer Female Pilot."

94. Williams, *Wasps*, 98.

95. Carl, *A WASP Among Eagles*, 52.

96. Williams, *Wasps*, 99.

97. Mondey, *American Aircraft of World War II*, 158–59.

98. Carl, *A WASP Among Eagles*, 53.

99. Williams, *Wasps*, 99.

100. Keil, *Those Wonderful Women*, 29.

101. Williams, *Wasps*, 102.

102. Ibid.

103. Keil, *Those Wonderful Women*, 288.

104. Schrader, *Sisters in Arms*, 180.

105. Keil, *Those Wonderful Women*, 218.

106. Ibid., 213.

107. Ibid., 213–17.

108. Ibid., 218.

109. Holbrook, "Coastside Woman."

110. Pohly, "Mabel Virginia Rawlinson."

111. Ibid.

112. Williams, *Wasps*, 136–37.

113. Jean, "Fallen Hero."

114. Keil, *Those Wonderful Women*, 232.

115. Merryman, *Clipped Wings*, 22.

116. Keil, *Those Wonderful Women*, 232.

117. Tekeei, "Fly Girl."

118. World War II Foundation, "Aircraft Facts."

119. Verges, *On Silver Wings*, 146–47.

120. Pisano, *Airplane in American Culture*, 175.

121. Kari, interview.

122. Keil, *Those Wonderful Women*, 184.

123. Ibid., 193–94.

124. Ibid., 184, 192–93, 204–5.

125. Schrader, *Sisters in Arms*, 181.

126. Tibbets, interview.

127. Collins, "Saint Paul–Born 'Fly Girl.'"

128. Strother, "Women of the WASP."

129. Keil, *Those Wonderful Women*, 282.

130. Ibid., 280–2.

131. Carl, *A WASP Among Eagles*, 59.

132. Ibid., 88.

133. Ibid., 61.

134. Ibid., 2.

135. Ibid.

136. Ibid., 101.

137. Ibid.

138 Arnold, "End of the WASP Program."

139. Yellin, *Our Mothers' War*, 161.

140. Williams, *Wasps*, 99–100.

141. Merryman, *Clipped Wings*, 55.

142. Schrader, *Sisters in Arms*, 246.

143. Schisgall, "Girls Deliver the Goods," 10.

144. *Life,* "Girl Pilots," 73–81.

145. Ibid.

146. Merryman, *Clipped Wings*, 58.

147. Ibid., 82.

148. Ibid., 82–88.

149. Comm. on Appropriations, H. R. Rep. No. 1606, 10.

150. Merryman, *Clipped Wings*, 90.

151. Ibid., 91.

152. Keil, *Those Wonderful Women*, 303–304

153. Merryman, 100.

154. Ibid., 23.

155. Rowley, "Teresa James: Pioneer Pilot."

156. Carl, *A WASP Among Eagles,* 111.

157. Williams, *Wasps*, 126.

158. Rowley, "Teresa James: Pioneer Pilot."

159. Williams, *Wasps*, 133.

160. Ibid., 41.

161. *Time*, "Army & Navy."

162. *WASP Final Flight* (blog), "WASP Betty Jane Williams."

163. *Deseret News*, "Death: Frances Green Kari."

164. Merryman, *Clipped Wings*, 130.

165. Ibid., 137.

166. Ibid., 138.

167. Yellin, *Our Mothers' War*, 161.

168. Williams, *Wasps*, 136.

169. Andy's WASP Web Pages, "Marie Muccie Genaro."

170. Merryman, *Clipped Wings,* 149.

171. Ibid., 155.

172. Ibid., 154.

173. Official Archive Women Airforce Service Pilots, "Assigned Duty Bases."

174. American Experience, *Fly Girls*, "Militarization of the Wasps." http://www.pbs.org/wgbh/amex/flygirls/peopleevents/pandeAMEX08.html.

175. Ricci, *WASP Newsletter*.

176. Merryman, *Clipped Wings*, 156.

177. Wolff, "Nicole 'Fifi' Malachowski."

178. Buzanowski, "Congressional Gold Medal."

179. Ibid.

180. Rowland, "Pioneer Female Pilot."

181. Grosscup, "Fly Girls."

182. Fandos, "Equal at Arlington."

183. Comulada, "Meet Elaine Harmon."

184. Grosscup, "Fly Girls."

Sidebar Text

*Garber, "Night Witches."

†US Department of Defense, "Description of Medals."

‡Lemmon, "Missing in Action."

§Pantti, "Gender, Politics and Media."

Time Line

Bold indicates WASP event

1939

September

World War II begins in Europe after Nazi armies invade Poland

Jacqueline Cochran writes letter suggesting women could fly in noncombat roles if needed

1940

April–June

Germany takes over much of western Europe

Nancy Love writes letter suggesting women could ferry planes in US

July

Germany begins air attacks on Britain

September

Germany, Italy, and Japan form Axis Alliance

US Congress begins nation's first peacetime draft

1941

March

US begins sending aid to Britain

June

General Hap Arnold suggests Cochran go to London to observe women military pilots there

Cochran becomes first woman to fly a military plane across the Atlantic Ocean

December

Japan attacks Pearl Harbor; US enters World War II on side of Allies

Cochran contacts women pilots about flying military planes in Britain

1942

March

Twenty-five American women begin training and flying in Britain under Cochran's supervision

June
After months of losses, US defeats Japan at Battle of Midway
July
Air Transport Command begins hiring civilian ferry pilots
September
Congress authorizes the Women Accepted for Volunteer Emergency Service (WAVES)
Nancy Love gets go-ahead to begin ferry pilot (WAFS) training in Delaware
Cochran gets go-ahead to begin broad training program (WFTD) in Texas

1943

February
WFTD training moves from Houston to Sweetwater, Texas
March
Cornelia Fort is first American woman military pilot killed on active duty
July
Women's Auxiliary Army Corps (WAAC) is militarized
WAFS and WFTD combine to form Women Airforce Service Pilots (WASP)

1944

March
Congress's Committee on Military Affairs recommends militarization for WASP
March–June
Columnists and male civilian pilots lobby against WASP
June
D-Day invasion reduces Allies' need for pilots
WASP militarization bill is defeated
December
WASP is disbanded without militarization

1945

May
Germany surrenders

August
Atomic bombs are dropped on Hiroshima and Nagasaki in Japan
September
Japan surrenders

1948
June
Women's Armed Services Integration Act makes women permanent, regular members of the military
July
Women in the Air Force are accepted for ground duty only and in limited numbers

1976
June
Women admitted to military service academies and accepted for pilot training
Former Wasps organize to demand militarization and veterans' benefits

1977
November
Congress passes and President Jimmy Carter signs bill giving the WASP military status

1984
WASP awarded World War II Victory Medals

2009
July
Congress passes and President Barack Obama signs a bill awarding the WASP the Congressional Gold Medal

Index

A

ace pilots, WWI fighter pilots, 83
African Americans
  migration changes, 39
  in military, 42
  Tuskegee Airmen, 64
  women pilots, 68
  in workforce, 41–42
Air Force. *See* United States Air
  Force (USAF)
Air Force Academy, 166, 173
Air Force Cross, 44
Air Force Reserve, 163, 168
air taxi service, 101, 111
Air Transport Command, 89
air travel
  beginning of, 4
  passenger plane exhibit, 6–7
airplane types
  AT-6 trainers, 86
  A-24 bomber, 109, 111
  B-17 (*See* B-17 bombers)
  B-24 bombers, 40
  B-29 Superfortress bombers,
    125–126, 127, 129
  B-34 bomber, 97
  BT-13 trainers, 80, 90–91
  C-60 cargo planes, 100
  gliders, 99–100
  jet propulsion engines,
    132–135
  P-39 Airacobra fighter, 86,
    118
  P-47 Thunderbolt fighter, 85
  P-51 Mustang fighter and
    fighter-bomber, 85, 87
  Piper Cubs, 106
  PQ-8 drones, 101
  PT-17 Stearman biplanes,
    88–89
  PT-19 trainers, 56, 67,
    87–88, 93
  T-6 trainer, 172
  target-practice planes, 61
airplanes
  beginning of, 4
  how they fly, 20, 133
  as weapons of mass
    destruction, 34
Allied alliance
  European progress (1943–

1944), 82
  Italy invasion, 81
  leaders of, 22
  members of, 22, 37
  Pacific front defeats, 49
  U.S. member of, 37
All-Woman Transcontinental Air
  Race, 163
altitude record, American
  women flyers, 15
American Airlines, 6
Arlington National Cemetery,
  175–177
Army Air Corps
  building resources for, 16
  creation of, 8, 49
  fighter plane escorts, 81–83
  need for planes, not pilots, 21
  noncombat flying jobs, 18, 51
  Plans Division, 19–20
  Women enlistment in, 45
Army Air Forces (AAF)
  African Americans in, 65–66
  bases and fields (*See specific*
    base and field by name)
  casualties, 49, 141
  congressional support for, 138
  flight school closings,
    141–142
  flight specialization, 83
  move from air war, 141
  on need for WASP program,
    150
Arnold, Bruce, 165–166, 167,
  168–169
Arnold, Henry "Hap"
  address to last WASP
    graduating class, 155
  death of, 165
  end of WASP program, 135
  Ferrying Command approval,
    51
  flying lessons for, 7
  halting trans-Atlantic flight,
    119
  as head of Army Air Corps,
    8, 49
  military flying approval, 61
  on need for larger plane, 125
  on need for planes, not
    pilots, 20

  on need for WASP program,
    150, 151
  on pilots for military, 48, 51,
    142, 166
  press reference regarding
    Cochran and, 151
  questioning women pilot's
    abilities, 21, 25
  testimony supporting Wasps,
    153
  White House aviation awards
    luncheon, 24–25
Aryans, defined, 10
Atlantic Ocean, air flights across,
  5, 116–119
atomic bomb, 129
Australia
  in Pacific front, 81
  pilots flying with RAF, 21
automobile plants, 38–39
Avenger Field, Sweetwater,
  Texas. *See* Women's Flying
  Training Detachment
  (WFTD)
awards and honors, 24–25, 44,
  149, 173, 175
Axis powers, 2, 22, 33, 35

B

B-17 bombers
  attacking Germany from
    England, 81
  on board bathroom, 121–122
  lost in battle, 115
  Memphis Belle, 153, 154
  Miss Patricia J, 114
  Queen Bee, 46
  size and strength of pilots,
    116–117, 120
  as test plane, 130
  training program, 119–122
B-24 bombers, 40
B-26 bombers, 123–125
B-29 Superfortress bombers,
  125–126, 127, 129
B-34 bombers, 97
barnstormers, 4–6, 56
bathroom issues, 63, 121–122,
  131–132
Batten, Bernice, 80
Battle of Midway (1942), 49

Battle of the Coral Sea (1942), 49
Baumgartner, Ann
  attitude after WASP's demise, 157
  background, 9–13, 22
  end of WASP program, 135
  as flight instructors after the war, 162
  Orville Wright meeting, 132–133
  target towing, 97–98
  test-fly first jet airplane, 134–135
  WASP training, 73–74, 76, 79
  Wright Field, Ohio, 130–132
beep pilots, 101–102
Bell Helicopter, 168
Bendix Trophy Race (1938), 15
Blue Angels, 170
boasting, bragging and, 17
bomber planes
  A-24, 109, 111
  B-17 (See B-17 bombers)
  B-26, 123–125
  B-29, 125, 129
  B-34, 97
  P-51 fighter-bomber, 85, 87
bragging, boasting and, 17
Britain. See Great Britain
British Air Transport Auxiliary (ATA), 26–27, 47, 49
British Royal Air Force (RAF), 21
Bronze Star, 44, 149
Brown, Willa, 68
Buckingham Army Air Field, Florida, 112
Burchfield, Phyllis, 54
burials, 91, 175–177
businesses
  household goods production, 162
  planning for war, 24, 38–39
  switch to military equipment, 160
  war-related businesses, 42
  women in workforce, 41

C

C-60 cargo planes, 100
Camp Davis, North Carolina
  abuse at, 152
  deaths at, 108–111
  maintenance problems at, 105–108
  monthly physical exams, 107
  morale at, 111–113
  photo of, 96

Canada, pilots flying with RAF, 21
Carter, Jimmy, 170
Chamberlain, Neville, 11
check pilots, 57, 76–77
China
  Allied alliance, 37
  Japanese land takeover, 33
Chinese American pilots, 65
Chrysler, 40
Churchill, Winston, 21–23, 40
Civil Aeronautics Administration (CAA), 127
Civilian Pilot Training Program (CPTP), 48, 54, 56, 67
Coast Guard Women's Reserve, 140
Cochran, Jacqueline
  on African American recruits, 65–66
  background, 15–19
  blamed for WASP's demise, 159–160
  on Camp Davis conditions, 106–107
  at class graduations, 79
  on conditions at Camp Davis, 111–113
  described in Life magazine, 146
  end of WASP program, 135
  flying to London, 25–26
  gag order, 142–143, 148
  Ninety-Nines member, 52
  photo of, 156
  plan for women pilots, 16, 18, 61, 99
  recruiting women pilots for ATA, 26–27, 47, 49
  support for, 160
  talk with Hap Arnold, 24
  target towing, 98
Cochran's Convent, 75
cohesion, 66
Coleman, Bessie, 68
college-educated women, 41
Combat Action Medals, 149
combat flying training, 62, 67
combat pilots, 48
combat positions, 149
communist countries, 22
Congress
  Committee on Appropriations, 150–151
  conscription act (draft) passed, 24
  declaration of war, 33, 35

investigation committee on WASP program, 149–150
men lobbying for WASP pilot jobs, 142, 148–149, 152–153
on militarizing WAFS, 54–55, 72, 137–138, 150, 152–153, 164, 171
military budget increase (1940s), 8, 24, 37
on military buildup (1920s and 1930s), 7
National Security Act (1947), 8
on veterans' benefits, 164
WASP Military Committee, 167–170, 175
WASP's burial at Arlington National Cemetery, 176–177
women in military academies, 166
women pilots for combat missions, 174
women's enlistment in military (1942), 42–43
Congressional Medal of Honor, 44, 173, 175
conscription act (draft), 24, 42, 142
Coral Sea, Battle of the (1942), 49

D

Dahl, Roald, 78–79
Defense Department. See Department of War
dehydration, 131–132
democracy, protection of, 13, 24
democratic countries, 2, 22
Department of Veterans Affairs, 175–176
Department of War (later Defense), 138, 148, 150
depression, economic disaster. See Great Depression (1930s)
dictators, 2
discharge papers, 169–170
Disney, Walt, 79
Distinguished Flying Cross, 44
Distinguished Service Cross, 44
Donahue, Barbara, 54
Dougherty, Dora, 113, 126–128, 163, 167–168, 176
draft (conscription act), 24, 42, 142
drill instruction, 58–59, 69–70
drones, 101–102
Dunkirk, France, 21, 22

E

Earhart, Amelia
  Atlantic Ocean, air flights across, 5
  disappearance of, 6
  as Ninety-Nines president, 19
  possible cause of death, 104
  solo flight from Hawaii to West Coast, 103
economic disaster (1930s). *See* Great Depression (1930s)
economic turn-around, 3
Ellington Field, Texas, combat pilots training, 62, 67
end of war issues, 140–141
Endeavor (space shuttle), 174
England. *See* Great Britain
Enola Gay (B-29), 129
Erickson, Barbara Jane "B.J."
  attitude after WASP's demise, 162
  competing in Powder Puff Derby, 163
  funeral service for Fort, 91
  love of flying, 162
  marathon ferrying, 84–85
  notifying families of deaths, 110
  photo of, 80
Ernst, Joni, 177
Europe
  German bombings, 23–24
  German invasions, 11, 21
  U.S. enters the war, 35
executive order, 39–40
experimental military test flights, 132

F

factories
  converting to military production, 24
  household goods production, 162
  mobilizing for war, 38–39
  switch to military equipment, 160
  women in workforce, 41
farmworkers, 41
Ferrying Command. See Women's Auxiliary Ferrying Squadron (WAFS)
ferrying planes
  bases for, 84, 94
  at Camp Davis, North Carolina, 96
  delivery statistics, 88–89
  marathon ferrying, 84–86

return trip transportation, 93–94
  risks, 89–93
  unscheduled landings, 86–88
  variety of planes, 83–84
  See also Fort, Cornelia
Fifinella, WASP mascot, 78–79, 127, 174
fighter planes
  British planes, 23–24, 81–83
  P-39 Airacobra, 86, 118
  P-47 Thunderbolt, 85
  P-51 Mustang, 85, 87
Fillmore, Carol, 87
film documentaries, 163
fireside chats, 36
588th Night Bomber Regiment (USSR), 26
Fleishman, Alfred, 70–72
flight instructors, 29, 30, 100–101, 119–122, 162
flight path, described, 20
Florsheim, Marion, 63–64
"flying coffin," 118
Flying Fortress. See B-17 bombers
"flying jalopies," 108
Ford Motor Company, 3, 40
Form One sheets, 106, 109, 110
formation flying, 90–91
Fort, Cornelia
  background, 29–30
  death of, 90–93
  desire to fly for military, 47–49
  as flight instructor, 29, 30
  on flight training completion, 59
  on New Castle training program, 56
  at Pearl Harbor, 31–33, 45
  photo of, 80
  recruited for Flying Command, 47, 52
  on the service of women pilots, 94–95
  WAFS member, 53
four-engine planes, 122, 126
France, Allied alliance, 22

G

gag order, 142–143, 148, 163–164
Gardner Field, California, 103
General Electric, 3, 162
General Motors, 3, 40
Germany

Axis alliance, 2, 22
  Britain bombings, 23–24
  declares war on U.S., 37
  European countries invaded, 11, 21
  Great Britain at war with, 11
  Luftwaffe, 48, 81
  as totalitarian government, 2
  U-boats, 12, 81, 98
  U.S. entrance in WWII, 40
  See also Hitler, Adolf
Gilbert Islands, 49
Gillies, Betty Huyler
  attitude after WASP's demise, 157, 162
  B-17 training and flying, 46, 116–117
  background, 52–53
  at Camp Davis, 113
  end of WASP program, 135
  flying large planes, 57–58
  flying tribute to Fort, 92–93
  as military drill instructor, 59
  New Castle training program, 55
  work after the war, 163
"Girl Pilots" (magazine article), 144, 147
glass ceiling, 119
glider towing, 99–100
Gold Medal recipients (2010), 174
gold star families, 92
Goldwater, Barry, 166
government jobs for women, 41, 42
Great Britain
  Allied alliance, 22
  Dunkirk battle, 21
  entrance into WWII, 11
  fighter plane escorts, 23–24, 81–83
  German bombings, 23–24
  North Africa victory, 81
  women pilot's program, 25–26, 47
Great Depression (1930s)
  economic slowdown, 2–3
  financial costs, 7
  managing bad news, 36
  stifled dreams, 6
  world-wide, 1–2
Great Migration, 39
Great War. *See* World War I (Great War)
Green, Frances, 119–122, 131
Greene, Betty, 130, 132

The Gremlins (Dahl), 78
The Gremlins (Disney book), 79
ground war focus, 141
Guadalcanal, victory in, 81
Guam
 Allies' defeat, 49
 Japanese attack, 35

H
Hanrahan, Marion, 107–110, 111
Harmon, Elaine, 172, 175,
 176–177
Harmon Trophy (1938, 1939), 17
heavy bombers, 122
helicopter pilots, 163
Helms, Susan, 174
Hiroshima, Japan, atomic bomb
 attack, 129
Hitler, Adolf
 growing tensions, 9–11
 military aggression threats, 1
 Nazi Party, 10
Hollingsworth, Lois, 102, 163
Holocaust, 10, 158
Hong Kong, 49
House of Representatives
 Committee on
 Appropriations, 150–151
 on militarizing WASPs, 150,
 152–153
household goods production,
 162
Huston, Texas, WFTD training
 program. *See* Women's
 Flying Training Detachment
 (WFTD)

I
imperialism, 2
industries
converting to military
 production, 24
growth and migration changes,
 39
household goods production,
 162
mobilizing for war, 38–40
switch to military equipment,
 160
women in workforce, 41
instrument flying skills, 99
Italy
 Allies' invasion, 81
 Axis alliance, 2, 22, 35
 declares war on U.S., 37
 as totalitarian government, 2
 U.S. entrance in WWII, 40

J
Jacqueline Cochran Cosmetics,
 17
James, Teresa, 85–86, 88,
 157–159, 162
Japan
 Axis alliance, 2, 22, 33
 China, land takeover,, 33
 Pearl Harbor attack, 28,
 31–34
 Southeast Asia, land
 takeover,, 33
 as totalitarian government, 2
 U.S. entrance in WWII, 40
Java (Indonesia island), 49
jet propulsion engine planes,
 132–135
Jews, in Germany, 10, 158
Jim Crow laws, 39
job variety for women pilots
 air taxi service, 101, 111
 assisting mechanics, 108
 commitment to, 61, 99
 flight instructors, 100–101
 flying redlined planes,
 105–106
 glider towing, 99–100
 maintenance testing, 103–105
 military pilots training, 101
 night flying, 99
 safety pilots, 102
 searchlight flying, 99
 target towing, 97–98, 165
 See also ferrying planes
jobs for WASP pilots after the
 war, 162–163
Johnson, Didi, 126–127

K
K rations, 38
Kellogg Company, 38
Kitty Hawk, North Carolina, 4

L
Ladies Courageous (movie), 145
Ladybird, B-29 Superfortress,
 127
LGBTQ in military, 66
Life (magazine), 136, 144–148
lift, air, 20
Lindbergh, Charles, 5, 6
Lockbourne Army Air Base,
 Ohio, 119
Long Beach Army Air Field,
 California, 84, 85, 90, 112, 152
Love, Nancy
 with 1930 circa plane, 14

advocate for recruiting
 women pilots, 19–20, 27
 B-17 training, 116–117
 B-17 trans-Atlantic flight,
 118–119
 background, 19
 end of WASP program, 135
 Ferrying Command approval,
 51
 Ferrying Command
 recruiting, 51–55
 fighter planes, 87
 at Fort's funeral, 91
 as military drill instructor,
 58–59
 on New Castle training
 program, 56
 Ninety-Nines club member, 19
 Queen Bee B-17 pilot, 46
 rooftop navigation points, 19
Luftwaffe, 48, 81

M
Malachowski, Nicole, 174
mascot, 78–79, 127, 174
McSally, Martha, 176–177
Memphis Belle, 153, 154
Menges, Kay, 111
Meserve, Gertrude, 57
Midway, Battle of (1942), 49
Midway Island, Japanese attack
 (1941), 35
migration changes, 39, 42
Mikulski, Barbara, 177
militarism, 2
militarization of women's service
 Appropriations Committee,
 150–151
 congressional position on,
 137–140
 30 years after the war,
 164–166
 timing of request for, 140
 for WAFS, 54
 for WASP, 72, 137–138
military
 African Americans in, 42
 foreign aggression threats, 1
 medals and honors, 44, 149,
 173, 175
 military budget increase, 8
 U.S. expansion of, 7, 16
 women's jobs in, 18, 41–43,
 48, 51
 See also specific military units
military academies, admitting
 women, 166, 173

Military Affairs Committee, 153
military auxiliaries, 140
military discipline, 167–168
military flying for women pilots, 61–62
military pilots training, 101
minority population, opportunities for, 41–42, 66
Mitchell, Logue, 119–122
monthly physical exams, 107
Morgan, Robert "Bob," 153, 154
mother ships, 101
Muccie, Marie, 70–71, 167
Mussolini, Benito, 35

N
Nagasaki, Japan, atomic bomb attack, 129
national cemeteries, 175–177
National Museum of the United States Air Force, 154
National Security Act (1947), 8
nationalism, 2
Native American pilots, 65, 68
navigation points, rooftops as, 19
Navy. *See* United States Navy
Navy Cross, 44
Nazi Holocaust, 10, 158
Nazi Party, 10
New Castle Army Air Base, Delaware. *See* Women's Auxiliary Ferrying Squadron (WAFS)
New World, called to help Britain, 23, 40
New York Times (newspaper), 1, 145
New York, World Trade Center terror attack, 34
New York World's Fair (1939-1940)
  jet engines, 132
  passenger plane exhibit, 6–7
  visitors to, 3, 21
  women's image, 3, 162
  "World of Tomorrow," x, 1, 3–4
  night flying, 99
Night Witches, 26
Nineteenth Amendment, U.S. Constitution, 161
Ninety-Nines (club for women flyers), 19, 52
noncombat military jobs, 18, 43, 51
Noonan, Fred, 5
North Africa, 35, 81, 174

Noyes, Blanche, 15
nuclear age, beginning of, 129
nurse corps, 43–44, 146

O
Obama, Barack, 175, 177
Odlum, Floyd, 17
Olds, Robert, 19–20
Order of the Fifinella, 164

P
P-39 Airacobra fighter, 86, 118
P-47 Thunderbolt fighter, 85
P-51 Mustang fighter and fighter-bomber, 85, 87
Pearl Harbor (1941), 28, 31–34
Pennsylvania, September 11, 2001 terror attack, 34
Pentagon, September 11, 2001 terror attack, 34
Philippines
  Allies' defeat, 49
  Japanese attack, 35, 49
physical exams, monthly, 107
physical training (PT), 68–69
pilots
  barnstormers, 4–6, 56
  early days, 6
  ferrying pilots (*See* ferrying planes)
  Ninety-Nines club, 19, 52
  regular AAF pilots, 83
  size and strength issues, 57–58, 69, 116–117, 120
  for tourists, 29
  training program, 30, 48
  women flying heavy planes, 25
  women volunteering during war, 18, 25–27
  women's jobs after the war, 162
  See also airplane types; *specific pilots by name*
Piper Cubs, airplanes, 106
Plans Division, Army Air Corps, 19–20
Poland, invasion of, 11
Poole, Barbara, 56, 87–88
Porter, Helen, 169–170
Powder Puff Derby, 163
PQ-8 drones, 101
precision flying teams, 170, 174
PT-17 Stearman biplanes, 88–89
PT-19 trainer planes, 56, 67, 87–88, 93
publications on women's war

efforts, 142–148, 151–152
public's view of women in the military, 147, 148, 151–152, 164
Purple Heart, 44, 149
pursuit planes, 85

Q
Queen Bee B-17, 46

R
racial integration, 66
racial segregation, 39, 65
racism, 10
radar, 19
Ramspeck, Robert, 149
Ramspeck Report, 149–152
Rawlinson, Mabel, 108–111
RCA, 3
records of WASP unit closed by government, 163, 168
redlined planes, 105–106
refueling missions, 173–174
refugee ships, 12
repaired planes, testing, 69
Robertson, Jeanne, 89
Rockwell, Norman, 139
Roosevelt, Eleanor, 17, 18–19, 51, 73
Roosevelt, Franklin D.
  address nation about Japanese attack, 35–36
  call for citizens to fight, 140
  on Churchill's call for New World help, 23
  death of, 129
  declared war on Japan, 33, 35
  executive order ending automobile production, 39–40
  fireside chats, 36
  Great Depression, relief during, 2–3
  military budget increase, 8
  military buildup, 16
  at New York World's Fair, 1, 3
Rosie the Riveter, 139
Russia. *See* Soviet Union (USSR)

S
sabotage, 111
safety pilots, 101–102
Saipan base, 125–126, 128
scapegoating, 10
searchlight flying, 99
September 11, 2001 terror attack, 34

sexual harassment, 77
Shaffer, Gene, 103–105, 162,
    177
Sharp, Evelyn, 56, 80
Silver Star, 44, 149
silver wings, 79
Singapore, 49
size and strength of pilots,
    57–58, 69, 116–117, 120
Slade, Shirley, 136, 146
Southeast Asia, Japanese land
    takeover, 33
Soviet Union (USSR)
    Allied alliance, 22
    stopped Germans in eastern
        Europe, 81
    women flying squadrons, 26
    WWII death toll, 158
SPARs, Coast Guard Women's
    Reserve, 140
Spirit of St. Louis (airplane), 5
Star Wars (movie), 167
Steele, Kaddy, 98, 164, 166, 175
stock market crash (1929), 2
strengthening exercises, 120
Strohfus, Betty Wall, 174–175
Strother Field, Kansas, 169
suffrage movement (1848), 161

T
target towing, 97–98, 165
television, introduction of, 3–4
test pilots, 103–105
testing center, 130
Thaden, Louise, 15
"The Girls Deliver the Goods"
    (newspaper article), 143–144
thrust, 20, 133
Thunderbirds, 170, 174
Tibbets, Paul, 126–127, 129, 153
Time (magazine), 157, 160
totalitarian governments, 2
totalitarianism, 2
Towne, Barbara, 80
trainer planes
    AT-6, 86
    BT-13, 80, 90–91
    PT-19, 56, 67, 87–88, 93
    T-6, 172
trans-Atlantic flight, 5, 116–119
truant officers, 107
Truman, Harry, 129
Tunner, William, 51, 106–107,
    116, 118
Tuskegee Airmen, 64
two-engine planes, 122
Tyce, Bob, 32

U
U-boats, 12, 81, 98
United States
    Allied alliance, 22
    North Africa victory, 81
    Pearl Harbor attack, 28,
        31–34
    WWII death toll, 158
United States Air Force (USAF)
    Air Force Academy, 166, 173
    Air Force Cross, 44
    Air Force Reserve, 163, 168
    establishment of, 8
    Thunderbirds, 170
    training women on military
        aircraft, 166
    Women in the Air Force unit,
        165
    women pilots, 165
    women's jobs in, 165
    See also Army Air Corps;
        Army Air Forces (AAF)
United States Armed Forces
    acceptance of African
        Americans and women,
        65–66
    expansion of, 37–38
    minority groups, 66
    precision flying teams, 170,
        174
    twenty-first century
        achievements, 149
    women pilots acceptance,
        173–174
United States Army
    Air Corps (*See* Army Air
        Corps)
    Air Forces (*See* Army Air
        Forces (AAF))
    Army Nurse Corps, 43–44
    Blue Angels, 170
    expansion of, 24, 37–38
    medals and honors, 44, 149,
        173, 175
    WFTD (*See* Women's
        Auxiliary Ferrying Squadron
        (WAFS))
    women pilots, 165
    Women's Army Corps, 8,
        137, 140
    Women's Land Army, 41
United States Constitution,
    Nineteenth Amendment, 161
United States Navy
    Blue Angels, 170
    medals and honors, 44
    Navy Nurse Corps, 43–44

WAVES units, 42–43, 137,
    140
    women pilots, 165
upward lift, 20
USS Shaw, 28
USSR. *See* Soviet Union (USSR)

V
Veterans Affairs Department,
    175–176
veterans benefits, 159, 164, 166,
    167, 171
victory gardens, 38

W
WAC (Women's Army Corps), 8,
    137, 140
wage difference, 41, 43, 54
Wake Island attacks, 35, 49
Walker, Mary Edwards, 44
Walt Disney Studios, 79
War Department, 138, 148, 150
war-related businesses, 42
washout rate, 76–77
WASP Military Committee,
    167–170, 175
    See also Women Airforce
        Service Pilots (WASP)
WAVES (Women Accepted
    for Voluntary Emergency
    Service), 42–43, 137, 140
West, Nadja, 149
Westinghouse Electric
    Company, 3, 139, 162
White House aviation awards
    luncheon (1941), 24–25
Williams, Betty Jane, 69, 79, 99,
    160, 163
Willow Run, Michigan, B-24
    bomber production, 40
women
    altitude record, 15
    awards and honors, 24–25,
        44, 149, 173, 175
    in combat, 66
    expected to give up wartime
        jobs, 162
    flying refueling missions,
        173–174
    in military, 141
    military academies admission,
        166, 173
    in powerful positions, 149
    in space flight, 174
    USAF's precision flying team,
        174
    in workforce, 41–42, 140–141

Women Accepted for Voluntary Emergency Service (WAVES), 42–43, 137, 140
Women Airforce Service Pilots (WASP)
  accident and fatality rate, 150
  Appropriations Committee, 150–151
  Arnold's address to last class, 155
  attitudes after WASP's demise, 157–160, 163
  Avenger Field training base, 72, 73
  barracks conditions, 74
  as a civilian program, 72, 91, 110
  congressional investigation committee, 149–150
  Congressional Medal of Honor, 173
  discharge papers, 169–170
  end of program, 135, 137–138, 153–154
  ferrying planes (*See* ferrying planes)
  flyboy's fake emergencies, 75
  formation of, 72
  gaining respect of male pilots, 113
  government closes records of, 163, 168
  graduation rate, 150
  job variety (*See* job variety for women pilots)
  lyrics for familiar songs, 77–78
  mascot, 78–79, 127, 174
  men lobbying for WASP pilot jobs, 142, 148–149, 152–153
  militarizing expectations, 72, 137–138
  militarizing request timing, 140–142
  military discipline, 167–168
  morale at Camp Davis, 111–113
  newspaper publication for trainees, 78
  non-traditional women's work, 138–139
  official recognition of military service, 171
  publicity of women pilots, 142–148
  Ramspeck Report, 149–152
  reputations rules, 75
  reunions, 164
  solo pilot recognition, 77
  training completion, 76
  training requirements, 72
  veterans benefits, 159, 164, 167, 171
  washout rate, 76–77
  See also Women's Auxiliary Ferrying Squadron (WAFS); Women's Flying Training Detachment (WFTD)
Women in the Air Force (WAF), 165
Women's Armed Services Integration Act (1948), 173
Women's Army Corps (WAC), 8, 137, 140
Women's Auxiliary Ferrying Squadron (WAFS)
  approval for women pilots, 51
  background of pilots, 53–54
  as a civilian program, 54–55
  cockpit training, 56–57
  flight uniforms and equipment, 59
  ground courses, 56
  instructors, 56–57
  marching in review with military units, 58–59
  merged into WASP program, 72
  militarizing expectations, 54
  photo of, 80
  pilots pulled for combat, 50
  qualifications, 53–54
  recruits, 51–55
  room inspections, 55–56
  women pilots recruiting effort, 51–53
Women's Flying Training Detachment (WFTD)
  approval for, 61
  Army life training, 71–72
  arriving at, 60
  backgrounds of trainees, 63–64
  as a civilian program, 62, 70
  clothing, 70–71
  drill instruction, 69–70
  instructors, 67–68
  merged into WASP program, 72
  move to Avenger Field, 60, 72
  physical training, 68–69
  qualifications, 62, 72
  racial diversity, 65
  testing repaired planes, 69
  training planes, use of, 67
  training program, 62–63, 67
  women pilots recruiting effort, 62
  See also Women Airforce Service Pilots (WASP)
Women's Land Army, 41
women's movement, 161
women's rights and opportunities, 5
"women's work," 138–139
Wood, Betty Taylor, 111
workforce changes, 41, 140
"World of Tomorrow" (N.Y. World's Fair theme), x, 3–4
World Trade Center, terror attack, 34
World War I (Great War)
  ace pilots, 83
  devastation during, 11
  migration changes, 39
  use of airplanes, 4, 7
  women volunteering pilots, 18
World War II
  Britain's entrance, 11
  causes, 2
  deadliest war in history, 158
  ground war focus, 141
  Hitler's responsibility for, 10
  migration changes, 39
  1940 Germany invades European countries, 21
  1942 Pacific front defeats and victories, 49–50
  1943 Europe and North Africa country's progress, 81
  1943 Pacific front victories, 81
  1944 attack on Japan, 125–126
  1944 war nearing end, 140
  U.S. entrance, 35–37
Wright brothers (Orville and Wilbur)
  Arnold's flying lessons with, 7
  first airplane (1903), 4
  Orville at Wright Field, 132–133, 153
  Wilbur, death of, 132
Wright Field, Ohio, 130–132, 153

Y
Yount, Martin, 144

Z
"zoot suits," 71